UNIVERSITY OF
WOLVERHAMPTON

SPECIAL EDUCATIONAL
NEEDS AND THE
NATIONAL CURRICULUM

Bedford Way Series
Published by Kogan Page in association with the Institute of Education
University of London

THE BEDFORD WAY SERIES

SPECIAL EDUCATIONAL NEEDS AND THE NATIONAL CURRICULUM

The Impact of the Education Reform Act

Edited by
HARRY DANIELS AND JEAN WARE

Contributors:
Ingrid Lunt, Brahm Norwich, Klaus Wedell,
Jannet Wright

KOGAN PAGE
Published in association with
The Institute of Education, University of London

First published in 1990 by Kogan Page Ltd,
120 Pentonville Road, London N1 9JN

Typeset by DP Photosetting, Aylesbury, Bucks
Printed and bound in Great Britain by
Biddles Ltd, Guildford

British Library Cataloguing in Publication Data

A CIP catalogue record for this book is available from the British Library.

ISBN 0-7494-0179-6

Contents

Notes on Contributors

All the contributors are members of the Department of Educational Psychology and Special Educational Needs at the Institute of Education, University of London. Klaus Wedell is Professor of Educational Psychology with reference to Children with Special Needs.

The particular teaching and research interests of the contributors are as follows:

Dr Harry Daniels Integration of children with special needs into mainstream schools; school organization; strategic approaches to mathematics in children with special educational needs; pupils' perception of schooling.

Ingrid Lunt Professional educational psychology; evaluation in education, especially school differences; integrated provision in mainstream schools; the National Curriculum and pupils with special educational needs.

Dr Brahm Norwich Curriculum issues in special education; the affective aspects of learning and teaching; psychological services for children.

Dr Jean Ware Education of children with severe, profound and multiple learning difficulties; staff–pupil interactions, classroom organization, curriculum development, integration.

Professor Klaus Wedell Policy and provision issues for children with special educational needs; component processes in basic educational attainments; objective-orientated approaches to teaching.

Jannet Wright Provision for children with communication problems; specific language disorders; language acquisition and development.

Preface

This collection of papers represents the thinking of a group of staff at the Institute of Education. Inevitably, in the years that followed the implementation of the 1981 Education Act, we have to some extent developed a shared view of appropriate ways to provide for children with special educational needs. The 1988 Education Reform Act with its provisions for the National Curriculum, has posed a severe challenge to our definitions of good practice. An analysis of special educational need formulated in terms of the provision required to make progress possible has been the basis of this practice. Definitions of progress and the principles of the management of systems of provision have been changed. In attempting to ensure quality of provision through a blend of competition between schools and regulation of practice within schools there is a danger that the Act will inhibit the flexible way in which individual teachers, schools and authorities have provided for the needs of individual pupils. We are concerned that the economics of competition between schools as governed by local-financial-management procedures may result in educational provision which is cost effective but not related to individual need.

In the context of such rapid educational change we felt that it was appropriate to pool our thoughts about the impact of the 1988 Act. The results of this exercise reveal a healthy tension between our respective positions that we felt might usefully be shared with a wider audience.

The focus of the collection is on aspects of the 1988 Act itself rather than on particular groups of children. It does not claim to be a complete review of the impact of the Act: the selection has been guided by individual interest rather than any other principle. Our aim was to provide a general overview along with more detailed analyses of the possible outcomes for groups and individuals who might be subjected to the National Curriculum exemption procedures; and also for the services which have a responsibility to provide for children with special educational needs. We have provided a digest of those sections of the Act dealing with disapplication and modification of the National Curriculum as an appendix.

Klaus Wedell brings to the introductory chapter the benefits of his experience of the House of Lords lobby during the passage of the Education Reform Bill. He provides an overview of the curriculum issues and also of the wider principles of regulation introduced by the Act. These are examined in greater detail in subsequent chapters. Harry Daniels, Jean Ware and Brahm Norwich explore the implications of the regulations governing disapplication and modification of the National Curriculum. The position of support services, both within education and provided by allied professions, is considered by Ingrid Lunt and Jannet Wright.

We hope that the collection will leave the reader with an impression of some of the tensions which will have to be resolved in practice and highlight the potential hazards for pupils with special educational needs and those who support them.

Harry Daniels and Jean Ware
Institute of Education
University of London
April 1990

Chapter One
Overview: The 1988 Act and Current Principles of Special Educational Needs

Klaus Wedell

The 1988 Education Reform Act and the subsequent flood of official pronouncements have given the impression of sweeping away the validity of existing principles and practice in education. The flood has appeared to threaten the steady and reasoned development of thinking and experience on which the principles have been built.

Few areas of education have seen such major developments over the last 20 years as special needs. Due to the pressure of public opinion, changes in the underlying principles and practice have been adopted in legislation and public-policy statements. Rather than allowing these principles to the swept away by the new pronouncements, it is important that the 1988 Act and the related official pronouncements should be evaluated in their light. I would like to attempt this in this introductory chapter.

Over the years, the new principles have been set out in the 1970 Education (Handicapped Children) Act, Department of Education and Science (DES) Circular 2/75, the Warnock Report (1978), the 1981 Act on Children with Special Educational Needs, DES Circular 1/83 (and its revision in Circular 22/89: DES, 1989b), three major DES-funded research projects, and a report from the Commons Select Committee on Education, Science and the Arts. These and other statements set out not only the radical change in thinking about what constitutes good education for children with special educational needs, but also how it should be provided.

Principles in the education of children with Special Needs
The main principles concerning education for children with special educational needs can be summarized as follows:

- Special educational needs are no longer seen as caused solely by factors *within* the child. They are recognized as the outcome of the interaction between the strengths and weaknesses of the child and the resources and deficiencies of the child's environment.
- It is therefore not meaningful or even possible to draw a clear dividing line which separates the 'handicapped' from the 'non-handicapped'. SENs occur across a continuum of degree.
- All children are entitled to education. The aims of education are the same for all children, but the means by which the aims can be attained differ, as does the extent to which they may be achieved.
- All schools have a responsibility to identify and meet children's special educational needs, and all children should be educated with their peers as long as their needs can be met, and it is practicable to do so.

Not only were the above principles formulated in legislation and other official pronouncements, but in recent years a good start was made in implementing them. This was shown by the findings from three DES-funded research projects, as well as from other research carried out since the 1981 Act came into force (Wedell et al, 1987). The findings showed, for example, that the majority of local education authorities (LEAs) allocated a higher proportion of their funds to developing provision for special needs; that new in-service training had resulted in more ordinary schools adopting relevant whole-school policies; that many special needs services devised new ways of providing support; and that special schools were breaking out from their segregation by building links of many kinds with ordinary schools.

The 1988 Act
Is the 1988 Act informed by these principles, and does it promote the development of good practice? The proposals originally put forward in the government's 1987 consultative document, and even the initial formulations of the Bill, were written with practically no regard to these principles and developments. Some amendments were made during the passage of the Bill, and subsequent circulars and other government documents have gone some way to revising the provisions of the Act. The National Curriculum Council (NCC) has also shown concern to apply the principles, especially in its pamphlet *A Curriculum for All* (NCC, 1989a).

One of the potentially positive points of the new legislation is its stress on the pupil's entitlement to a 'broad and balanced curriculum'. From the point of view of special-needs education, the following questions need to be asked:

- Who is entitled to the curriculum?
- What is the entitlement curriculum?
- How are pupils with SENs able to gain access to it?

Who is entitled to the curriculum?

Those concerned with the education of children with special educational needs tried, during the passage of the Bill, to have the word 'all' inserted in Section 1, so as to make it quite clear that this entitlement extended to all children at a school. Although this amendment was repeatedly refused by the government, the point was apparently recognized later, because it has been emphasized by italics in the Government's booklet *From Policy to Practice* (DES, 1989a).

The National Curriculum part of the 'broad and balanced' curriculum is specified for pupils within the 5–16 age range. It therefore does not cover children below or above school age, although the NCC's non-statutory advice for primary schools includes advice about 'rising fives'. Whether or not the National Curriculum covers the attainment levels of those pupils who are within the compulsory school age range but are not achieving the requirements of level-1 attainments seems to be a matter of controversy. At the time of writing, this has not been officially resolved, and clearly leaves a big question about how the National Curriculum is intended to serve this section of the school population.

What is the entitlement curriculum?

As far as content is concerned, the Act gives pupils an entitlement to a 'broad and balanced' curriculum, but it only *specifies* those parts of the curriculum represented by the subject-based National Curriculum (religious education is not specified in this way). The former HM Senior Chief Inspector of Schools Sheila Browne is reported to have said at the time of the passage of the Bill through parliament that 'there is a considerable gap between the core and foundation subjects in terms of which the National Curriculum is described in the Bill, and the aims stated in clause 1 of the Bill'. Others also made similar criticisms of the limited concept of curriculum promoted by the Act (Fish et al, 1987, 1988). This view of the curriculum is unfortunate for all pupils, but particularly so for those with special educational needs which have to be met by a broad curriculum offering. Here again, subsequent non-statutory pronouncements by the government indicate that the point has been noted: 'the foundation subjects are certainly *not* a complete curriculum' (original italic, DES 1989a). In the same document there is a reference to alternative ways of thinking about curriculum content 'helpfully' provided by HMI. The NCC has also shown concern that other conceptions of curriculum content should be promoted (NCC, 1989a).

Although it is to be hoped that these further formulations will correct some of the shortcomings of the way in which the curriculum is promoted by the Act, it must be recognized that, as the Circulars of Guidance are careful to emphasize, only the content of the Act has the force of law.

At a minimal level the prescription of the coverage of ten subjects does make a contribution in those instances where pupils with special educational needs have not been provided with such an offering. This has sometimes happened in both special and ordinary schools, partly because of staff shortages. The introduction of the National Curriculum has certainly highlighted such shortages, though at the time of writing there is no indication of a successful solution.

The Act and the relevant circulars have also provided an emphasis on progression through the ten levels of the attainment targets for each subject. The subject working parties have stressed that their formulation of the content and progression in each subject have to be regarded as a best first effort; this is hardly surprising considering the diversity of views about curricular content. In fact, there has been remarkable acceptance of the suggested formulations, and this is no doubt due to the non-specific way in which they have been expressed. However, the very fact that teachers have been challenged by these formulations to consider the content and progression of subject matter has been a significant contribution. The analysis of content has been a major activity among teachers involved in special needs education, since they are constantly having to clarify for themselves what the specific elements of subject content are, and to break down the subject progression into smaller learning steps. It has also formed the basis of teachers' curriculum-based assessment (CBA).

The curriculum working parties were aware that the ten levels for all subjects recommended by the Task Group on Assessment and Testings (TGAT), might not necessarily fit the progression of each subject or the attainment targets within them. For example, the most meaningful analysis of a subject might not allow it to be divided into ten successive sections, let alone equal sections. Consequently, although all working parties presented attainment targets divided into ten levels, one cannot assume that these are necessarily equal steps of progress. Although special needs teachers will use the levels as a benchmark in their CBA, they may well find the need to analyse the content differently in planning the next steps for a pupil.

The entitlement curriculum also includes assessment within the subjects of the National Curriculum at the four key stages. It seems, from the general pronouncements which have referred to assessment, that this is to be carried out with reference to the ten levels of each of the attainment targets (Schools Examination and Assessment Council, 1990). It has also been proposed that children's achievement should be aggregated into the profile components within subjects, or into aggregate attainment-target levels for a complete subject. The assumption is that in each subject the ten levels can now be equated with normative achievement levels at the successive ages of pupils within the compulsory school age range. The curriculum working parties no doubt kept this in mind in formulating the ten levels within attainment targets. Up to the present, there is of course no evidence to support the validity of this norm-referencing, and so the levels will have to be used as a rule of thumb, and one will have to hope that the levels in different attainment targets correspond.

Assessment is only worthwhile if it provides useful information. The 1988 Act and the associated documents mention three purposes of assessment: to help the teacher choose the next step for teaching; to provide parents with information about their child's progress; and to provide aggregate data to evaluate the quality of education offered by the school.

The Act only refers to assessment at the four key stages: 7, 11, 14 and 16. These involve teacher assessments and Standard Assessment Tasks (SATs) aimed at producing individual and aggregate data.

As far as the teacher's CBA for choosing the next step for the pupil is concerned, it seems obvious that the assessments at key stages will be too widely spaced in time to provide the rate of feedback a teacher needs in day-to-day teaching. This can only be achieved through on-going CBA, related now, on a rule-of-thumb basis, to the levels within the attainment targets.

The information which parents want about their children, particularly if they have special educational needs, will also need to be derived from ongoing curriculum-based assessment. Parents will not want to wait between one key stage and the next to find out how their children are progressing; this is recognized in the draft circular covering section 22 of the Act. Parents may also want to know how their children are progressing in relation to their age. Since key-stage assessments will be too widely spaced, teachers will presumably refer to the rule-of-thumb levels of the attainment targets.

The third purpose of assessment mentioned in the Act and other documentation is the assessment of the quality of education offered by schools based on the aggregate performance of pupils in a school at each key stage. The Schools Examination and Assessment Council has indicated the problems of deriving an aggregated achievement for a pupil from the proposed teacher assessments and SATs, particularly if SATs are to be modified or disapplied for some pupils (Schools Examination and Assessment Council, 1989). There are major doubts about how valid the derivation of aggregate data can be, let alone the economics of achieving any adequately moderated assessment.

None the less, there is no question that the quality of education offered needs to be assessed, though the government's commitment to this does seem in doubt. In *From Policy to Practice*, the DES states that the achievement levels of pupils with special needs should be assessed, but that their assessment data need not be included in the published aggregations so that 'schools need have no fear that the overall picture of attainment for their pupils will suffer because children with special needs are included' (DES 1989a, para. 8). Are schools not to be evaluated on the quality of education offered to *all* their pupils?

How are pupils with SENs able to gain access to the curriculum?
The Act and the associated circulars do make an attempt to allow for flexibility in applying the National Curriculum to meeting individual needs. Provision for this is made in sections 4, 17, 18 and 19.

Section 4 requires the Secretary of State to prescribe the content of the subjects of the National Curriculum by issuing 'orders'. In doing so, he has also used the opportunity in the accompanying circular (Circular 6/89) to make provisions for how the curriculum should be applied. Each of the subject formulations produced so far have made reference to how pupils with special educational needs might be served, although the scope provided for flexibility is not intended to apply solely to such pupils. The circulars for example, recognize that, within any key-stage, pupils' attainment will range over different levels. The 'ranges [of levels within the key stages] indicate the extent of differentiation which may be required: they do not indicate that *all* the programme of study material within the ranges should be taught to all or even most pupils within the key stage in question' (Department of Education and Science, 1989c).

Schools are allowed to 'teach the pupil for part of the time at a level falling outside the key stage.' This 'part of the time' may amount to 'half or more', so long as the pupils work within the key stage levels 'during the latter part of the key stage'. It is envisaged that a 'pupil may be moved . . . down a key stage for the subject in question, by placing him or her in a teaching group in which the pupils are . . . younger'. Not surprisingly, the NCC comment that 'this option will not often be practicable or educationally desirable' (National Curriculum Council, 1989a).

All these provisions indicate that the National Curriculum is to be applied in a flexible way, and it is claimed that the scope for making these variations will make it unnecessary to increase the number of pupils with statements. On the one hand, these comments are welcome because they seem to recognize that current good practice in flexible teaching to meet pupils' needs can be continued. On the other hand, they raise questions about whether the Act will in fact increase a pupil's 'entitlement' to the National Curriculum, since all this 'flexibility' can be offered without the accountability assured, for example, by the statement procedure.

The wording of these circulars does not provide a teacher with any additional basis for deciding when a modification of the National Curriculum is so extensive that it is 'infringing' a pupil's entitlement.

Sections 17 to 19 of the Act are intended to cover the instances where it is felt that the National Curriculum should be modified or 'disapplied' to meet a pupil's needs to such an extent that formal accountability measures are required. These sections are described in Circular 5/89 as offering 'a package of provisions designed to accommodate pupils' particular needs' (DES, 1989) not only special educational needs. Section 17 is aimed at general formulations referring to 'cases and circumstances' in which such accommodation might be required. However, it seems widely agreed that it would be difficult to make such formulations in an educationally meaningful way. So far, the only instance cited refers to pupils who have progressed beyond level 10 of the National Curriculum before the age of 16.

Section 18 deals with disapplication and modification within the 1981 Act statement procedure. This section does not change the principle of specifying in a statement how children's needs should be met, but it does require that a positive recommendation should be made whenever a modification or disapplication of the National Curriculum is proposed.

Section 19 gives powers to headteachers temporarily to disapply or modify a pupil's curriculum. The headteacher does not have to seek specialist advice before using these powers, as is required for statement recommendations. There is considerable unease about whether this section will always be used for the benefit of the pupil. Circular 22/89 emphasises that the section should be invoked sparingly, and with due discretion (DES, 1989b).

Surprisingly, the three sections fail to distinguish how they relate to the three separate aspects of the National Curriculum enumerated in section 2(2) of the 1988 Act – the attainment targets, the programmes of study and the assessment arrangements at key stages.

Attainment targets

The principles of special needs education mentioned at the beginning of the chapter would lead a school to avoid disapplying any attainment target in its entirety. On the other hand, the earlier discussion has shown that it will not be easy to decide when 'informal' modifications of attainment targets and programmes of study turn into formal modifications and disapplications.

Programmes of study

It seems obvious that programmes of study might have to be modified or disapplied, but only in order to help individual pupils with special educational needs to achieve the attainment targets. The NCC has provided guidance about this in its booklet (NCC, 1989a), and the orders also make a few suggestions related mainly to pupils with sensory and motor disabilities.

Key-stage assessments

Because the Act only refers to assessment in terms of the key-stage procedures, sections 17 to 19 can only refer to assessment in these terms. There are references in the circulars on the curriculum issued so far under section 4 orders, to ways in which the assessment measures should allow for pupils' special educational needs as far as possible. The most obvious relevance of these provisions is to sensory-motor and communication impairments. Major complications are involved in assessing pupils who are working at levels below their age-appropriate key stage because of the procedural provisions of the Act and circulars. So far, there have been no suggestions as to how these complications can be circumvented, but one would hope that pupils will not be disadvantaged as a result.

The issue of disapplying assessments for pupils with special educational needs has already been raised. If it is regarded as inappropriate to disapply an aspect of the National Curriculum from a pupil, then it would follow that it is inappropriate that a school's performance in that area of teaching should not be evaluated.

The provisions for implementing the Act still leave many questions unanswered about access for children with special educational needs to the National Curriculum, let alone to a 'broad and balanced' curriculum. None the less, it seems likely that access may well be limited less by the provisions of the National Curriculum than by the administrative provisions of the Act.

Administrative considerations

Many of the administrative provisions of the Act have direct or indirect implications for the education of pupils with special educational needs. It has been said that, given goodwill, there is no need for the implementation of the Act to put the advances in meeting pupils' special educational needs at any risk. However, presumably the purpose of legislation is to prevent bad consequences as much as to foster good ones. Furthermore, at times of constrained resources, good will may not be enough to ensure that choices are made in favour of pupils with special educational needs.

The government's admission in *From Policy to Practice* that schools may be anxious about publishing the achievement results of pupils with special educational needs indicates that it is itself aware that the Secretary of State's wish to introduce competition between schools may affect their commitment to such pupils.

At a time of constrained resources, schools will be placed in a conflict about allocating effective support for pupils with special educational needs and, indeed, about admitting them. There are already indications of increased demands for special schooling, and even the links between ordinary and special schools are being put in doubt.

In its report on the implementation of the 1981 Act the Select Committee on Education, Science and the Arts stated that services for pupils with special educational needs were too complex to be left to schools to provide on their own. Yet the provisions of Local Management of Schools (LMS) for formula funding encourage such delegation of services, while explicitly recognizing that this may put the provision of support at risk.

The policies represented by the 1988 Act are directed at extending parental choice. In principle this is to be welcomed. However, the implications of such a policy differ very much in circumstances of sufficient and insufficient resources. In general, one would presume that parents want the best for all children, not just their own. But when resources are constrained or non-existent, parents not unnaturally are likely to put their own children's welfare before that of others. By definition, parents of children with special educational needs are in a minority. It is therefore not surprising that Baroness Warnock is reported to have said in connection with children with special educational needs, that one cannot leave it to parents alone to ensure that all children receive a proper education.

Conclusion

It is hardly surprising in view of the points considered in this chapter, that those with responsibility for the education of children with special educational needs view the potential consequences of the 1988 Act with apprehension.

The principle of the interactive causation of special educational needs was obviously not sufficiently considered by those originally responsible for drafting the Act. Awareness of the continuum of special educational needs, which range from profound and multiple disabilities to difficulties of a mild, moderate or temporary kind (NCC, 1989a), has provided the basis for building in some of the subsequent provisions for flexibility in implementing the National Curriculum. Although one of the main tenets of the Act is the individual's entitlement to a broad and balanced curriculum, the points raised in this chapter show that this may be applied in a partial and uncertain way for pupils with special educational needs. There is no doubt that the provisions of the Act make it more difficult for schools to comply with the 1981 Act requirements that schools should meet the special educational needs of their pupils, and further the process of integration.

Teachers and other professionals concerned will no doubt do their utmost to protect children from the potential negative consequences of the 1988 Act – though at a time of impaired professional morale and limited allocation of finance, this will not be easy to achieve. Both professionals and parents will need to be vigilant in order to identify those aspects of the implementation of the Act which are jeopardizing the chances of providing a proper education for children with special educational needs.

Chapter Two
The National Curriculum for Pupils with Severe Learning Difficulties

Jean Ware

In all its 284 pages the 1988 Education Reform Act makes no mention of specific categories of pupils (except those being educated in hospital schools) who should or can be exempted from the National Curriculum. The assumption is that *all* pupils should receive not only the National Curriculum, but a curriculum which is balanced and broadly based. However, four sections within the Act enable the National Curriculum to be modified or disapplied on a temporary or more permanent basis (sections 16–19). Two of these sections, 16 and 17, apply to groups of pupils, and two sections, 18 and 19, to individuals. There is no exemption from section 1 (the requirement that all pupils shall receive a balanced and broadly based curriculum).

Section 16 is not intended to make provision for pupils with special educational needs but to allow for 'educational experiments'; it therefore provides for whole schools to be exempted on a temporary basis for this purpose. Section 17 is presumably intended to enable the Secretary of State to exempt whole categories of pupils from the National Curriculum, or parts of it. It has been clear since the Bill was first mooted that the pupils most likely to be the subject of such a group exemption are those with severe learning difficulties (SLD), and it is the application of the National Curriculum to this group that forms the focus of this chapter.

Initially the view of experts in the field was that the National Curriculum was unlikely to be applied to schools for such pupils and that it would not be appropriate for them. However, as it has become clear that the National Curriculum is being seen more and more as an entitlement curriculum, more and more of those working with children with severe learning difficulties have turned their attention to the problem of how the National Curriculum might be applied to their pupils. In part, as for other pupils with special educational needs, this change of attitude represents a pragmatic approach. If we're stuck with it we have a duty to our pupils to make the best of it. But for pupils with severe learning difficulties, there are also other factors playing a part. Not least of these is a fear that to argue that the National Curriculum should not apply to these pupils as a group would be to argue them out of their hard-won and so far short-lived place in the education system. In this context, it is significant that it is still only in the USA, Canada, and Britain that even the most profoundly handicapped pupils are entitled to state education, but also that in all these countries the heady optimism which followed their admission has largely given way to a recognition of the difficulty of the task. For example, in 1989 a bill was laid before the Canadian Parliament to re-exclude those with profound and multiple learning difficulties (PMLD) from the education system. Additionally, there is strong social pressure on all those concerned with pupils with special educational needs not to be seen to be arguing for a segregationist viewpoint.

However, this does not neutralize the two fundamental questions which form the basis of this chapter:

- Can we implement the National Curriculum for pupils with severe learning difficulties?
- Should we implement the National Curriculum for pupils with severe learning difficulties?

It seems to me that the answer to neither of these questions is the forgone affirmative that much recent writing on the topic seems to assume. Unless we address these questions honestly, we stand to do a grave disservice not only to children with severe learning difficulties but to *all* children.

Can we implement the National Curriculum for pupils with severe learning difficulties?

What do we mean by 'implement the National Curriculum'?

There has been a great tendency for those who work in the SLD field to regard this question as an invitation to demonstrate that activities can be provided for pupils with severe learning difficulties which can be seen as 'working towards' the attainment targets of the National Curriculum. Consequently there has been a proliferation of material (much of it unpublished) designed to show that the curriculum currently in use in our SLD schools already provides work related to many of these attainment targets (eg Tilstone and Steel, 1989). Most of this work uses a process which has become known as 'mapping' – that is, it takes the school's current curriculum documentation and the attainment targets for one of the National Curriculum core areas and proceeds to demonstrate that many of the attainment targets (at least at levels 1–3) already appear in different words as objectives in the school's curriculum. Once those targets which already appear have been identified, the missing ones are added. Alternatively, in good SLD tradition, the process starts with an individual child, examines their daily or weekly timetable and identifies those curriculum targets that the child is already working on. Again, those not present are added (eg, Tilstone, 1989). By either of these procedures the school ends up with a reworded but substantially unchanged curriculum. These authors consider that they have demonstrated that the National Curriculum not only *can* be implemented with pupils with severe learning difficulties, but (with a few additions and alterations) is already being implemented.

There are, however, a number of problems with this approach. First, merely adding those attainment targets which were not previously included in the school's curriculum fails to address the issue of why they were originally omitted. Obviously it is possible that some of these additional targets represent a genuine and valuable broadening of the curriculum available to pupils with severe learning difficulties, but it seems unlikely that this is the case for more than a small percentage of the additional material. In most cases the people who have developed the curricula currently being followed in SLD schools are highly skilled and dedicated practitioners who have thought long and hard about what to include and what to omit.

Second, demonstrating that some or even most, attainment targets at the lower levels are being taught to some children in our SLD schools is not sufficient to fulfil even the general requirement of the Education Reform Act that *each* child must receive a broad and balanced curriculum:

> The principle that each pupil should have a broad and balanced curriculum which is also relevant to his or her particular needs is now established in law . . . That principle must be reflected in the curriculum of every pupil. It is not enough for such a curriculum to be offered by the school: it must be fully taken up by each individual pupil. (DES, 1989a, chapter 2)

Parts of what already appear as objectives in the curricula of SLD schools may be attained by only a tiny number of the most able pupils before school-leaving age and much of it may be taught to only a proportion of the pupils. Indeed if all pupils are to receive an education which is 'appropriate to their age, aptitude and ability' the most advanced objectives will necessarily apply to only a few of the school's pupils. This of course ought to have been true of any school operating under the 1944 Act. Therefore, showing that most of the National Curriculum is covered by that offered by SLD schools is not the same as showing that it can be implemented with all, or even most, pupils with severe learning difficulties. On the other hand, it probably does provide a sufficient demonstration that it would be inappropriate to use section 17 to exempt pupils with severe learning difficulties from the National Curriculum as a group.

More seriously, given the extremely wide ability range of pupils being educated in SLD schools, there is in all such schools at least a small group of pupils who currently attain few, if any, of the curriculum objectives outlined for the school as a whole. This group of pupils, the most severely handicapped, is already seen by many school staff as presenting a problem in terms of appropriate curriculum provision, and is sometimes even perceived as being 'off the bottom' of the *current* SLD curricula (Evans and Ware, 1987). In an attempt to meet the very special needs of this group of pupils, a growing number of schools are already providing them with an alternative curriculum, often described as 'a sensory curriculum' (eg Longhorn, 1988).

Within many SLD schools, there is another sub-group of pupils whose education is widely recognized as presenting particularly intractable problems: those described as having 'challenging behaviour'. During some periods of their schooling such pupils may spend large portions of the day engaged in intensive programmes designed to modify their behaviour, on the justifiable grounds that their most urgent need is to learn not to injure themselves. It has been argued that within the context of the National Curriculum such programmes could be seen as analogous to additional time spent learning braille by a blind child – that is, they promote curriculum access. In reality, however, unlike the blind child, many of these pupils will continue to need intensive programmes at intervals throughout their lives, some of them because their behaviour is associated with their handicapping condition, and some because in the current state of knowledge even the most skilled help is not always successful in enabling their problems to be overcome.

Furthermore, as Fordham has suggested, these two groups overlap with a number of pupils within SLD schools who may never attain any targets at Level 1 (Fordham, 1989). It does not matter that this group is a tiny percentage of the school population. For them, for their parents and teachers, the fact that they will potentially be 'working towards' the same curriculum targets throughout their school lives raises the painful issue of the extent to which they will *really* be receiving the National Curriculum.

Third, it is abundantly clear that when the National Curriculum is referred to in a mainstream context, or by DES personnel, what is meant is the curriculum and its associated assessment procedures. Arguably at least, it cannot be claimed that the National Curriculum is being implemented with pupils with severe learning difficulties unless this includes the assessment procedures – and there has been little discussion of how this might be achieved. Indeed, at least some of the literature which has emanated from the DES suggests that it is not considering assessing pupils with severe learning difficulties in the same way as other pupils (Fordham, 1989), while *From Policy to Practice* mentions disapplication of the assessment arrangements as one form of modification to the National Curriculum which may be appropriate to some pupils with special educational needs. At the very least pupils with severe learning difficulties will require statements allowing them to work more than one key stage below their chronological age.

It is not at all clear, therefore, that the National Curriculum can be implemented in any real sense for *all* pupils with severe learning difficulties, or that it can be implemented in its entirety for any of them. However, that does not necessarily mean that it cannot be implemented in a modified form. Indeed, I have suggested elsewhere that the main problem in implementing the National Curriculum for pupils with severe learning difficulties (particularly those with the most severe handicaps) lies in the linear conceptualization of progress that it seems to embody. If pupils could return to particular attainment targets at different times in their school careers, working on them at successively more complex levels, then even those with profound and multiple learning difficulties might legitimately be said to be learning about, for example, hypothesis testing. More importantly this might well be the most important thing for them to be learning in order to meet their priority needs.

Should the National Curriculum be implemented with pupils with severe learning difficulties?

It is easy to forget that the National Curriculum is only supposed to be a part of the whole curriculum, and that its implementation needs to be seen in the context of the overall aim of the Act which is to provide a curriculum which:

(a) Promotes the spiritual, moral, cultural, mental and physical development of the pupils at the school and of society; and

(b) prepares such pupils for the opportunities, responsibilities and experiences of adult life. (*Education Reform Act, 1988*, p1)

It should be remembered that no exceptions are permitted.

It may be that for some pupils this overriding aim is best achieved by some means other than implementing the National Curriculum either in whole or in part. I should like to suggest that in our concern to prevent the marginalization of pupils with severe learning difficulties we have become overconcerned with the implementation of the National Curriculum to the detriment of this more fundamental aim. *It may be* the case that for pupils with severe learning difficulties, just as *it may be* the case for other pupils, that the best way to achieve this aim is through the National Curriculum; but in my view that is still an open question. There are several reasons for suggesting that this is in fact not the case.

First, it could be argued that for many pupils with severe learning difficulties the opportunities and responsibilities of adult life are likely to be so different to those of the 'average' pupil that alternative curriculum experiences are necessary to prepare them for that adult life. This is unlikely to be a popular point of view, since it goes against much of the current thinking in the area of normalization. Nevertheless, it must be considered. For example, the concept of 'planned dependency' has recently become popular in some quarters as a relevant and realistic aim for pupils with profound and multiple learning difficulties; this stands in sharp contrast to the current emphasis for most pupils on the cultivation of an 'entrepreneurial spirit'. On the other hand, there are elements of the personal and social education curriculum, particularly those concerned with consideration for others and being able to see things from the other person's point of view, which could be seen as equally relevant to mainstream pupils as to those with profound and multiple learning difficulties, forming an essential part of responsible adulthood for both groups, and already included in preparation for planned dependency. However, personal and social education is neither a core nor a foundation subject within the National Curriculum.

Second, for the most part those aspects of the National Curriculum which have generally been omitted from the curricula of SLD schools, have been left out only after careful thought and often much heart searching. As was made abundantly clear when the National Curriculum was first proposed and seemed likely to be in force for 90 per cent of the school day, everything that is included in the curriculum for any child means the exclusion of something else. It is a regrettable but unavoidable fact that pupils with severe learning difficulties learn very much more slowly than the majority of their peers. Effectively, therefore, they have much less time available to them for learning than other pupils, and the decisions about what they should be taught become both more salient and, arguably, more critical. Expert opinion is divided as to whether teaching should concentrate on developing a high level of skill in those areas which are essential to surviving in the adult community, or whether there should be more emphasis on developmentally appropriate activities. There is no disagreement about the fundamental point that time is at a premium, and decisions about what to teach have to be made.

There are, then, both advantages and disadvantages to implementing the National Curriculum with pupils with severe learning difficulties. The only advantage of wholesale (indiscriminate) implementation, however, would seem to be that it provides the best available safeguard against the marginalization of those pupils and their eventual re-exclusion from the education system. This does not, however, seem to be sufficient grounds for subjecting some pupils to a curriculum which manifestly fails to meet their most pressing needs. It is my considered view, however unfashionable or apparently reactionary, that there are undoubtedly some individual pupils whose needs would be better met by an exemption from the National Curriculum and the provision of a more appropriate alternative. This does not mean, however, that I am arguing for the use of section 17. To exempt whole categories of pupils (such as those with severe learning difficulties and challenging behaviour, or those with profound and multiple learning difficulties) would be to return to the era between 1944 and 1970, when all those with severe learning difficulties were deemed unsuitable for education in school. We should be prepared to fight fiercely for the right of every child to receive a curriculum which is individually tailored to their individual needs. For all pupils with severe learning difficulties this is likely to mean a degree of modification of the National Curriculum, and

for some the provision, at least on a temporary basis, of an alternative
to it.

Chapter Three
How an Entitlement can Become a Restraint

Brahm Norwich

Since the government first made its proposals about a national curriculum in 1987 there has been considerable uncertainty and anxiety about its relevance for and its effects on the education of children with special educational needs (SEN). It is possible to speculate about two phases in the response from those concerned with SEN to the introduction of the National Curriculum. The first involved an initial opposition (and some panic) expressed in terms of worst outcome predictions. As the Act has been implemented with the necessary involvement of teachers and educationalists, there has been some softening of the criticism as some of the worst fears were dealt with by the working parties. The second phase has involved a necessary coming-to-terms with the reform and even some positive perceptions of the benefits for children with special educational needs. This last phase could be seen as a sensible response to a *fait accompli*. However, it would be regrettable if the necessity to provide an educational service in the context of the 1988 Act had the effect of clouding clear ideas and judgements about what kind of National Curriculum framework is desirable for children with special educational needs.

My intention in this chapter is to consider the official central-government approach to the relevance of the National Curriculum to children with special educational needs. I shall argue that despite positive statements about, and arrangements for, including such children, there has been a notable lack of specific and practical guidance on when the National Curriculum is relevant. The recent National Curriculum Council document on special educational needs, *A Curriculum for All* (NCC, 1989a), is useful in terms of its positive approach to inclusion, and its practical suggestions for the classroom use of the core subject attainment targets and levels. Yet, it says little about the differing balances needed between the various parts of the National Curriculum and between the National Curriculum and a school's overall curriculum, and fails to take account of differences between individuals and between special and ordinary schools. I shall argue that this fundamental issue of curricular balance arises out of the purposes for which the National Curriculum was designed, namely, to make possible nationally comparable and publicly reportable assessment. I will develop this line of argument using the case of special schools for emotional and behavioural difficulties as an example.

The official line

Recent publications from the DES and the NCC, as mentioned above, reflect many positive approaches to SEN developed over the last two decades (DES, 1989; NCC, 1989a, 1989b). There has been recognition of the contextual nature of SEN, that learning difficulties arise out of the interaction of child and environmental factors. It is officially recognized that all pupils are entitled to receive the National Curriculum and that maximum participation requires good practice for all, which can be promoted through whole-school policies. Greater participation is also seen to be facilitated by the way in which attainment targets, programmes of study and assessment arrangements are formulated. A minimal use of the provisions for statutory exception (sections 17, 18 and 19) is also advocated.

Another way in which flexibility has been built into the National Curriculum has been in the specification of the range of attainment levels expected in each key stage (section 4 orders for maths and science, DES, 1989c) (see Table 3.1).

Table 3.1 *Range of attainment levels for the key stages for maths and science*

Key stage	Age range	Attainment level ranges	
		maths	*science*
1	5–7	1–3	1–3
2	8–11	2–6	2–5
3	12–14	3–7	3–8
4	15–16	4–10	4–10

Circular 6/89, which gives guidance on these section 4 orders, states that the great majority of pupils are expected to fall within these specified levels (DES, 1989c). Any further flexibility which may be needed could be made, according to the circular, without a statutory exception (section-18 exception) by:

- teaching a pupil for part of the time at a level outside the key stage range (paragraph 36i); or
- placing a pupil in a teaching group in which the majority of pupils are older or younger (paragraph 36ii).

It is interesting to note that the NCC has expressed doubt about the practicability and desirability of this second type of flexibility (NCC, 1989a). If any further changes are needed, then exceptions to the National Curriculum can be specified via section 18 in statements of SEN.

The need for specific official guidance

As I have agrued in a recent article (Norwich, 1989), the official position leaves all those concerned with the implementation of the National Curriculum for children with special educational needs in some uncertainty. For instance, at what point do the informal flexibilities mentioned in paragraph 36 of Circular 6/89, require the statutory exceptions as recorded in a statement? Circular 22/89, which replaced guidance on the operation of statutory assessment and the issuing of statements under the 1981 Education Act, refers to individual exceptions to the National Curriculum under section 18. However, in making it possible to have statutory exceptions to any or all of the requirements of the National Curriculum via a statement, there is no specification of what can or cannot be modified or exempted (disapplied).

The effect of this lack of specific guidance is to leave it to individual schools and LEAs to clarify these matters. This places considerable onus on LEAs and schools to make decisions without the benefit of a national perspective to support their implementation of the National Curriculum. This is likely to lead to a diversity of practice in making exceptions which may be unacceptable to parents, teachers and others interested in the education of children with special educational needs. It is also out of line with the trend towards more national specification about the curriculum. All that has been stated officially is that where exceptions are made there has to be an alternative to replace the exempted parts. What these alternatives might include has not been specified.

What is needed is guidance about how the different aspects of the National Curriculum can and should be adapted. This guidance would distinguish between informal exceptions, such as those mentioned in paragraph 36 of Circular 6/89 and formal exceptions as in sections 17 to 19 of the 1988 Act. Such guidance would also address questions about the focus and duration of formal exceptions. There have been regulations and a circular (15/89) about the operation of section-19 temporary exceptions, but here as elsewhere there has been little about the nature of the distinction between modification and exemption (disapplication). As these are the two central kinds of exception they need to be introduced in a way that makes their meaning clear and usable in the practical context of implementing the National Curriculum. Such clarification would identify how modification and exemption relate to different aspects of the National Curriculum. For example, is it appropriate in certain limited cases to exempt some of the foundation subjects but not the core subjects?

This leads to further questions about which parts of subjects (attainment targets) and over which key stages of schooling it is appropriate to modify or exempt. The question of whether exceptions apply some components of the National Curriculum and not others has also to be addressed. Is it, for example, appropriate to modify attainment levels, but not programmes of study and assessment arrangements, for some key stages but not for others?

In raising these questions about specific national guidance it is interesting to consider how this situation has come about. It is difficult to give definitive answers here but several possibilities can be considered. The one which is often given is that SEN is a low priority in the DES approach to the national education service and that mainstream considerations have dominated official interests. It is also worth considering that providing specific national guidance on SEN adaptations is an intrinsically complicated task and that without prior experience of implementing a national curriculum, it might be advisable to issue guidance after there has been some local experience of the National Curriculum with SEN. However, if this were the official line then it might be more reassuring to those charged with implementing the National Curriculum to be told in an open and frank manner.

There is still another aspect to the lack of official guidance. This concerns the wider context and ethos in the SEN field. The 1981 Education Act is commonly seen to reflect the abandonment of categories of educational handicap. This is often taken to imply that it is not possible to specify exactly when a child has a learning difficulty, because of the influence of contextual factors. This perspective is sometimes referred to as 'relativity', since it assumes that learning difficulties are relative to local educational standards and contexts. A radical relativity view would imply that it would be neither possible nor desirable to specify in general terms when and how exceptions to the National Curriculum are to be made. Even from a less radical perspective, it might be thought that to establish general categories and conditions for these National Curriculum exceptions would be to return to pre-1981 Act approaches.

However, as I have argued elsewhere (Norwich, 1990) it is mistaken to presume that the 1981 Education Act did actually abandon categories. What the legislation did was to abandon medical categories in favour of educational ones, such as learning difficulties. This is embodied in the Warnock Report's emphasis on assessing learning difficulties in individual terms which distinguish between deficits and their impact, influenced by other child and environmental factors on learning progress. This approach is not only consistent with, but requires, differentiation, that is, categorization, of the degrees and forms of special educational needs and provision. This point needs to be seen in the context of recent experience that one of the main issues in implementing the 1981 Act has been over how learning difficulties are identified and special educational needs are specified (Goacher et al, 1988). These difficulties are likely to be compounded by the use of the National Curriculum in the context of the 1981 Act without further clarification about how SENs are to be identified in National Curriculum terms.

Inclusion in the National Curriculum

Terms like participation and inclusion are used in the wider educational context in a value-laden way. As applied to children with special educational needs they reflect a strong commitment to making education relevant and appropriate to all children. Put in these terms, nobody could reasonably be opposed to the participation and inclusion of children with special educational needs. There could be no justification for excluding some children: to do so would be to signal an educational rejection and devaluation. This is the commitment which underpins the prescription in the Warnock Report that the purpose or aims of education are the same for all children.

One of the great challenges in actually formulating educational aims relevant to all children is that there is a need to balance the inclusiveness of the aims against their interpretability in concrete terms. The more inclusive, the less content they have; the more content, the less inclusive. Whatever balance is struck however, it is widely held that common aims do not require that more specific intended outcomes (ie goals and objectives) and methods would be the same for all. It is compatible with common aims to have some different goals, objectives and methods for some children, so long as these different means and short-term ends are themselves ways of meeting the inclusive general aims.

Following this line of argument, it makes sense to specify nationally a common curriculum framework for all children. A national curriculum which enables all children to participate in a common framework of learning therefore has clear benefits. The difficulty with the 1988 Education Reform Act version of a national curriculum is that it has been designed without much consideration of common aims – neither their inclusiveness nor their interpretation in terms of more specific areas of learning and experience. The 1988 Act has been designed mainly for accountability purposes and this has required that its design be influenced mainly by assessment and reporting considerations. The current National Curriculum can therefore be seen as assessment-led. The gap between the very general aim that the school curriculum should be balanced and broadly based and the selection of ten National Curriculum subjects as content areas illustrates the point. Much of the recent deliberations about the nature and design of the school curriculum were ignored in the National Curriculum design process.

Another design feature of the current National Curriculum has been that subject areas fit a ten-level progression through the target areas of learning. This design feature derives from the requirement that all learning and attainment be assessable in comparable form, so that it can be reportable for accountability reasons in a standard and relatively simple format. Any consideration that some areas of learning do not lend themselves to the standard ten-level scheme did not seem to be given serious consideration.

Differences in curricular balance

With the current National Curriculum, the range of subjects is likely to take up the majority of available time for school learning. Though this could be seen positively in terms of providing a common breadth for all children, such breadth could be at the expense of balance between different elements of the school curriculum for different localities and children. This question of accommodating some flexibility in curricular balance is at the heart of the relevance of the 1988 Act for the diversity of children in our society. It is one matter to favour a common framework and areas of learning for all children, it is another matter to prescribe in detail a common balance between the areas for all children.

The only way to combine some commonality of areas with some flexibility in balance between these areas is to prevent the areas taking up most of the available school timetable. Where this does not happen, what is offered as an entitlement to all can turn into a rigid restraint for some. It follows from this that if a common entitlement is to be relevant to some children with special educational needs, there needs to be more flexibility in the design and implementation of the National Curriculum.

In proposing that individual differences – particularly for children with the most exceptional needs – call for differences in curricular balance from the prescribed mainstream one, it is worth considering the kinds of different balances required. The first may arise from the need for more time to be spent on some curricular areas, perhaps because learning progress is slower in these areas (they may be considered priority areas, such as the core subjects of the National Curriculum). A second kind of balance difference may arise from the need for learning in areas not included in the National Curriculum or in the cross-curricular themes referred to by the NCC. This may be to enable curricular access, such as independence training for those with visual impairments.

A third kind of balance difference may arise from the need to give a more explicit emphasis and place to what are currently called cross-curricular dimensions and skills. This has particular relevance to the education of children with intellectual, emotional and behavioural difficulties. For children with intellectual difficulties it may be relevant and appropriate, following Feuerstein's instrumental enrichment approach (Feuerstein et al, 1979), to make some use of the space for the direct training of intellectual and problem-solving strategies and skills. Deficiencies in such cross-curricular skills are at the root of learning difficulties and may warrant both a direct and an integrated place in the curriculum for some children with special educational needs. The point here is not to advocate instrumental enrichment as such, but to illustrate the point that cross-curricular skills may need additional emphasis for some children with special educational needs.

Curricular balance for children with emotional and behavioural difficulties

Another example of the need for an additional emphasis on a cross-curricular dimension is the area of personal and social education for children with emotional and behavioural difficulties in special schools and units. For these children it may be relevant and appropriate to make additional timetable space for social skills and group work, for outdoor activities and pursuits which encourage trust between pupils and adults, and for personal counselling opportunities. One of the risks in pursuing this line of argument is that it could be seen to lead to the traditional opposition between therapeutic and educational approaches in this field. This is not the intention, as it has been argued above that children with emotional and behavioural difficulties would participate in the common curriculum. Nor is it proposed that an additional emphasis on personal and social education implies any commitment to curative therapeutic goals. This emphasis is part of a broader view of special needs education which also includes rehabilitative or corrective approaches when they are feasible and effective. The position taken here is that there is an unclear boundary between therapeutic and educational goals and methods and that it is not useful to make a fine distinction when it comes to designing programmes for children with emotional and behavioural difficulties in special schools and units. Emotional and behavioural development or growth (education) is not easily distinguished from emotional and behavioural readjustment (therapy).

There are grounds for reasonable disagreement about the exact balance between explicit personal and social education programmes and other elements of a special school curriculum. However, there are likely to be simple time constraints on the possibility of introducing such programmes into a school curriculum where the National Curriculum takes up the majority of available time. It is in this respect that there can be serious doubts about the relevance of all the ten subjects of the National Curriculum to special schools for children with emotional and behavioural difficulties. This position has to be distinguished from the one which considers National Curriculum exceptions because of widespread special school staff shortages for a subject area, such as foreign languages. The reason for doing so is that there could be similar shortages of appropriately trained and skilled staff to cover the personal and social educational needs of these children.

As argued in the first section, there is a need for national consideration and guidance on the matter of how modifications and exemptions relate to different National Curriculum subjects, different phases of schooling and different elements of the National Curriculum. This can be seen to be particularly relevant to the way in which special schools and units implement the National Curriculum. This position has focused mainly on the area of emotional and behavioural difficulties but similar points can be made for other areas of special educational needs.

Concluding comments

It has been argued that the National Curriculum resulting from the 1988 Act is not the only way to embody the entitlement of all children to a common curricular framework. It is not even the only important factor in so doing, because entitlement requires sufficient and appropriate staff and other resources to make it come about. When children bring different characteristics – strengths and weaknesses – to school learning, this calls for some flexibility in the selection of and balance between the common areas of learning. The need for flexibility in curricular balance is not only relevant to children with special educational needs, it is relevant to all children to some degree. However, it is particularly relevant to children who are exceptional in some way.

It is possible that the current ethos within special needs education will continue to reflect a clinging to oversimplified concepts of entitlement and a common curriculum. This is already evident in the move to avoid practical consideration of exempting some children with more severe difficulties in school learning from aspects of the National Curriculum. This avoidance is supportable at this stage in implementing the National Curriculum because the available attainment targets can be widely used in special schools. However, as the national assessment arrangements begin to come into operation it is likely to become more apparent that children who are learning at below level 1 cannot be included in the arrangements. At this stage, exceptions to the assessment arrangements will probably be required. Similarly, when certain foundation subject areas come into operation it is likely to become apparent that it may be neither feasible nor desirable to include certain subjects.

A final point concerns the effect of implementing the 1988 Act on special-needs education more generally. The National Curriculum is a centrally directed initiative which involves the tightening up of what is taught in schools and how learning is assessed. Implementing such an initiative in the context of the Local Management of Schools is likely to make extensive demands on the workings of the 1981 Education Act. It is likely to call for greater clarity about when an LEA will determine the additional or different provision needed for some children with special educational needs, that is, when to issue a statement. It is also likely to call for greater clarity about how special educational needs are described and provided for. It might even lead to a movement to amend and refine certain aspects of the 1981 Education Act.

Chapter Four
Implications for Special Educational Needs in the Ordinary School

Harry Daniels

This chapter aims to present an overview of some of the possible implications for children with special educational needs (SEN) in ordinary schools of section 19 of the 1988 Act. The possibilities afforded by the practice of temporary exception using section 19 of the Act will be considered in detail. This will involve an examination of regulations which are complex and advice which appears to be contradictory. To explore these possibilities I will consider the position of children with special educational needs in an unsympathetic school in an unsympathetic borough. The intention is to reveal what could be the worst possible case and in so doing set priorities for pre-emptive action.

This analysis will be conducted against the background of the recent experience of the implementation of the 1981 Education Act. This has revealed a high degree of variation in local education authority (LEA) policy and practice with respect to appeals, availability of information, composition of appeals committees, time taken to process statements and many other aspects (Goacher et al, 1988). An experience which suggests that predictions of worst possible cases are too often fulfilled.

Competition between schools

When the Secretary of State for Education introduced the ideology of competition into the public provision of education with the 1988 Act, he also created a number of regulations governing a new economy of schooling. Competition is being promoted as the new dynamic that will stimulate better standards. One of the avowed intentions of the Act was to encourage schools to compete with one another for limited resources – pupils. The quality of education offered in a school would, it was argued, be enhanced as a consequence of this competition.

A demand led, consumer-oriented system such as the one created by the implementation of the 1988 Act requires incentives to stimulate competition. The major incentive for competing schools is the money made available under Local Management of Schools (LMS) schemes, all of which calculate school budgets on the basis of numbers of children on roll. Open enrolment will increase the competition between schools for pupils. One of the mechanisms by which schools will advertise their worth, and thereby enter into the educational marketplace, is through the publication of their aggregated academic achievements. Marketing through the publication of aggregated subject scores and description of resources available to pupils may become a significant part of the economic activity of schools. The increasing number of 'marketing for schools' in-service training courses suggests that this is already the case.

This marketing of schools could be used to promote the image of state schools in the face of strong private-sector competition. However, as Doe (1989) noted in his *Times Educational Supplement* article ('To market, to market, to sell a fine school'), there is considerable conflict surrounding the issue as to who should market schools and concern as to the basis on which schools should be marketed.

The proposed publication by each school of aggregated subject scores may well prove to be of importance within the economy of the wider community. There has always been an unofficial school-catchment-area effect on house prices, based on local qualitative evaluations of school worth. Publication of quantitative data in the form of subject attainments will provide the consumers – parents – with what would appear to be a more reliable basis for discriminating between schools. In the American system, local academic profiles are presented on property details by estate agents!

Certainly, the pressure on schools to present the best possible public image will be considerable. This could lead to overall improvement in the system as judged by attainment-target criteria. However, there is also the worrying possibility that children whose performance at key stages would not make a positive contribution to the school's aggregated position in the local educational market economy will have only restricted access to the National Curriculum. The 1988 Act defines the details of the curriculum to which all children are entitled, yet also provides a number of mechanisms for restricting access or even denying that right. Disapplication and modification of the National Curriculum provide what could prove to be a rather too attractive method of removing children from the database from which school attainments are aggregated. A brief examination of the literature reveals that this possibility has been recognized. However this recognition has not led to the formation of a consistent set of conclusions concerning the significance of the process.

Conflicting influences?

There is an apparent conflict between some of the agencies involved in the development of the National Curriculum with respect to policy on children with special educational needs. The Department of Education and Science (DES) does not appear to be entirely in agreement with the National Curriculum Council (NCC). According to the DES document *From Policy to Practice*, which was distributed to every serving teacher, one of the benefits of disapplying or modifying all or any part of the National Curriculum for pupils with special educational needs is as follows:

> 'That way schools need have no *fear* that the overall picture of attainment for their pupils will suffer because children with special educational needs are included.' (DES, 1989a, para 8.5, my italic)

As details of the process of aggregation and publication are not yet available it remains a matter of speculation as to how this 'benefit' would be realized and also as to whether reference is being made to pupils with or without statements of their needs. However, the use of the word *fear* does suggest that the writers of this document were under the impression that children with special educational needs constituted a threat to the public image of the school. The suggestion that fear of this threat may be removed by some aspect of disapplication or modification is echoed by a concern expressed by the NCC in their non-statutory guidelines for the implementation of the National Curriculum for children with special educational needs:

> No ordinary schools should be *tempted* to use the statementing procedures as a pretext for transferring certain pupils to special schools or units merely because they are not expected to perform well on national assessments at 7, 11, 14, 16. This would be in conflict with the aims of the 1981 Education Act which has not been superseded by the Education Reform Act. (NCC 1989a, p 11, my italic)

Interestingly what was seen as a benefit in the case of the former becomes a temptation in the latter. Whether this difference in orientation towards the process of making exceptional arrangements for pupils with special educational needs reveals the existence of more fundamental differences between the respective organizations is as yet unclear. However, there are other suggestions that this is the case. While the Secretary of State has spoken of the need to foster *competition* between schools in order to ensure quality of provision, the NCC has written of the need to promote *cooperation*:

> Much planning is needed to enable all pupils with SEN to benefit from the National Curriculum. Vital aspects of this will include cooperation within and between schools in developing policies and practice; regular information to, and active involvement of, parents and governors; and support from specialists in LEAs. (NCC, 1989b, para 13)

Clearly, there are conflicts of orientation at very senior levels. As a result, schools will be receiving conflicting messages about how they should behave towards children with special educational needs. This situation could allow a pattern of highly localized interpretations of legislation to take place during the implementation of the 1988 Act similar to that observed during the implementation of the 1981 Act, (Goacher et al, 1988). There is, therefore, the potential for what must be taken as the benevolent intentions of the legislators to be abused under local social and economic pressure. The possibilities afforded by sections 16, 17 and 18 are explored in this volume by my colleagues Jean Ware and Brahm Norwich. It is section 19 of the 1988 Act which is to be considered here. This is the section which provides for temporary exceptions from the National Curriculum and is the subject of Circular 15/89. It constitutes the major concern, in terms of formal exceptions, for the position of pupils with special educational needs in mainstream schools in local education authorities where there is little commitment to the aims of the 1981 Act. The importance of section 19 is increased by the recent changes in the statutory procedures under the 1981 Act, (DES, 1989b). Circular 22/89 announces that while the Secretary of State expects that children in special schools would normally be afforded the protection of a statement, it is thought that statements may not be needed in mainstream schools. This allows for a larger domain of decision-making within which local pressures may operate than was the case under Circular 1/83 (DES, 1983).

It is possible that a number of children with special educational needs will find themselves subject to informal exceptions to the National Curriculum. Circular 6/89 (paragraph 36) allows children to be taught outside their expected key stage for part of the subject time in their own classes, or with children outside their key stage for whole subjects,

(DES, 1989c). While this allows for the possibility of the creation of some unusual forms of vertical grouping it does not allow for reporting requirements to be lifted. It does, of course, suggest that the extinct 'remedial', 'special' or 'progress' class could be revived. The regulations available for scrutiny at the point of writing suggest that teaching outside expected key stage may be organized on an informal basis with no recourse to complaints or review procedures. However, if the requirement of the school is to avoid the fearful effects of low attainments being revealed in published aggregated scores, then section 19 deserves closer attention.

Section 19

A headteacher can invoke section 19 to remove a child from the National Curriculum and thus the assessment arrangements, for an initial period of up to six months and up to one year on renewal. In that LEAs will define the sort of variations in special needs between schools which should be taken account of in their formula for the distribution of financial resources (DES, 1988b para 155), it may be that there are economic as well as marketing incentives for invoking section 19. As Coopers and Lybrand noted in their report on Local Management of Schools, if a high level of resources is allocated for such pupils schools, may seek a classification of pupils to maximize their overall level of resources, (section 3.18). This may apply for statemented and non-statemented pupils alike.

Section 19 allows for temporary exceptions to be made in certain conditions but does not *require* them to be made in these conditions. The definition offered of these conditions is given in very general terms relating to the pupil's circumstances or conduct. These conditions of circumstances or conduct *could* be seen to apply in a large number of cases. Two types of direction may be made under section 19. The first is a general direction given when factors necessitating the exception are likely to have changed in six months. The second type is a special direction made when it is felt that the pupil has longer-term needs and that these will have to be met through a statement. The analysis in this chapter is with respect to general directions.

The Secretary of State suggests that section 19 should not be widely used. Circular 15/89 emphasizes that the provisions for exemption should be applied sensitively and positively and that positive alternatives should be offered in all cases. This expectation of rare and sensitive use of exceptional arrangements is advocated by both the NCC and the DES. Indeed the Secretary of State has announced the intention to monitor use of section 19 by means of a new DES return (DES, 1989d). The question that awaits an empirical answer is how the DES would respond to an LEA which was considered to be abusing section 19.

At another level of control, section 8(2)c of the 1944 Act was amended by the 1981 Act to place a duty on LEAs to 'have regard to the need for securing that special educational provision is made for pupils who have SEN' (Education Act, 1981). This should allow LEAs the right to inspect a school with respect to use of section 19. Again, the questions that await answers concern the extent to which LEAs will act against schools in their use of section 19. The answers to some of these questions may have to be sought in the courts. Guidance in circulars does not constitute authoritative legal interpretation of any Act; that is exclusively a matter for the courts.

The circular on temporary exceptions (DES, 1989d) states that the Secretary of State expects headteachers to discuss the pupil's circumstances and needs with his or her parents and teachers and consult medical officers, educational psychologists or other specialist staff before giving a direction of temporary exemption, (para 23). Circular 22/89 also requires schools to publish information for parents indicating their special support provision for children with special educational needs, but with no statements, (DES 1989b, para 16). The suggestion was made by the National Curriculum Council (NCC, 1989a) that exceptions should not be made to the National Curriculum for children with learning difficulties as a way of manipulating school attainment profiles. Schools were warned that such a practice would embody an inherent contradiction with the aims of the 1981 Act. This suggestion would appear to lack a biting edge in the face of evidence that these aims have already been contradicted by existing practice. Some LEAs have shown somewhat less affiliation to the aims of the 1981 Act than others. Presumably they will not feel inhibited about promoting actions that compound their position with respect to these aims. A school that is anxious to attract as many pupils as possible under open enrolment in the face of stiff competition will wish to present as polished an image of the institution as possible. Temporary exception within six months of the assessment point for a key stage could provide a strategy for improving the attainment profile of the school. Whilst this suggestion may be thought of as being somewhat over-pessimistic, past experience of the implementation of educational legislation has demonstrated that any loophole will be exploited (Goacher et al, 1988).

Appeals

Clearly, safeguards are needed within the system of management of section 19. In order to preserve what has become generally accepted as good practice since the implementation of the 1981 Act it will be of paramount importance to ensure that children's access to the curriculum to which they are entitled is not blocked. Circular 22/89, section 22, clearly states that the 1988 Act aims to raise the expectations of *all* pupils (DES, 1989b). Section 19 could be abused by schools and LEAs who – for political, economic or ideological reasons – do not subscribe to the principles of equality of educational opportunity espoused by the Warnock Report (which in turn were refined by the ILEA's Fish Report). Children could be disenfranchised from their educational entitlement by the cynical actions of organizations motivated solely by the incentives of the market economy of LMS and open enrolment. The importance of parental appeals against the misuse of section 19 is clear.

DES Circular 1/89 issued on 9 January 1989 outlines advice to LEAs on the establishment of local arrangements for the consideration of complaints and invites them to submit their proposals to the Secretary of State. Four stages of appeal are proposed (DES, 1989e):

- Stage 1 involves informal discussion with teachers and headteachers. Circular 15/89, issued on 11 July 1989, suggests that a headteacher should allow one month between giving and implementing directions under section 19 for parents and the LEA to query the reasons, to object or ask for changes.
- Stage 2 involves a formal complaints procedure the details of which will be formulated by LEAs. In the first instance this will be referred to the governing body, the same governing body responsible for local financial management.
- Stage 3 involves referral to the LEA using section 23 of the 1988 Act and the subsequent involvement of the local appeals machinery.
- Stage 4 involves referral to the Secretary of State under sections 68 or 99 of the 1944 Education Act.

There are some interesting criteria for the handling of complaints given in Annexe of Circular 1/89 (ibid). One of these is that there should be a clear point of contact within the LEA for formal section-23 complaints. Given the variation between LEAs in information available concerning the 1981 Act it is vital that this information becomes widely available.

Annexe A further suggests that there should be a 'mechanism to identify all *relevant* complaints and weed out those not within the scope of Section 23' (Annexe A section 5 (ii)). A strange use of language in so sensitive a context! All LEAs have now submitted plans to the DES which detail how they intend to satisfy the criterion of 'weeding out'. It would seem important to ensure that this process is carried out in an unbiased way.

LEAs are to be obliged to inform complainants of the reasons for decisions taken and also about the next stage of the process. They will also be expected to identify urgent cases, deal with them appropriately and report to governing bodies, Education Committees and the DES the number of complaints dealt with, their outcomes and the time taken to deal with them. Clearly, in the case of temporary action under section 19, time is of the essence. As soon as children are removed from the National Curriculum they will inevitably start to drift away from the curriculum position of their peers. The longer this happens, the greater the curriculum distance will be and the more difficult it will be for the child to reintegrate.

Safeguards against long spans of temporary periods of exception are suggested in Circular 15/89 (DES, 1989d). There are two possibilities for extended periods of temporary exception, these being the renewal of an existing direction and the issue of further new directions under section 19. A headteacher may renew an initial exception on up to two occasions for a maximum of three further months in each case. This may only be done with the written permission of three governors in the first case and the written permission of the LEA and the governors in the second case. Only three governors have to sanction these extensions because other members of the same governing body may be involved in the appeal procedures. An interesting example of self-regulation!

A pupil who has already been the subject of a direction under section 19 may be issued with a new order of temporary exception. This may be within a year of the expiry of a previous direction if the governors, (another subgroup!, Circular 15/89 para 46) and the LEA give their written consent.

The involvement of the LEA in these renewals and new directions should act as a safeguard against over-zealous use of section 19 in schools tempted to remove large numbers of low-attaining pupils from their aggregated attainment scores as a ploy to maintain a favourable position in the local educational marketplace. The situation will need careful monitoring.

Effective use of appeals procedures should help to prevent unfair practice arising. Unfortunately there is no guidance as to the constitution of the local appeals committees. Under the 1981 Act LEAs were seen to vary considerably in the way they constituted appeals committees. The appeals committees set to operate under section 23 of the 1988 Act will be responsible for a wide range of appeals outside the special educational needs field. It will be by no means certain that any member of these committees will be suitably informed as to the SEN issues that obtain.

If the restricted headway made by the 1981 Act is to be maintained and enriched by the positive aspects of the 1988 Act there is much to be done. Close scrutiny of local parental appeals procedures is vital. In this respect there is an important role for parental support groups and advocates. They would do well to explore the practice that arises from the suggestion in DES Circular 22/89 (1989b), para 16, that schools should publish information for parents indicating their special support for children with special educational needs but no statements. Perhaps this could even become part of the marketing strategy of schools trying to attract the so-called middle ground, particularly as the NCC (1989a) has recently reiterated the position established in the Fish Report (ILEA, 1985b) with respect to the general value of good practice:

> Schools that successfully meet the demands of a diverse range of needs through agreed policies on teaching and learning approaches are invariably effective in meeting special educational needs. (NCC, 1989a para 5)

If the government's true pupose is to create a better educational system for *all* children then it too must play some part in ensuring that the system it has created is not abused. The DES will be faced with the task of responding to their monitoring of the use of section 19.

LEAs will have the task of monitoring the use of section 19 in their schools. It seems quite possible that an LEA will have to take a school to court. This would arise when a school driven by the pressures of marketing in an unpredictable economy has to resort to a system which generates unequal opportunities.

Those working in the system will need to ensure that the parents of pupils subject to section 19 know of their rights and are encouraged to exercise them.

Unfortunately, it would appear that some of the concerns raised by this chapter are manifesting themselves. Doyle and Rickman (1989) report the reactions of a group of headteachers to the prospect of paying for pupils with special educational needs under LMS:

SENs are, almost of necessity, becoming a low priority in planning at school level . . . while only headteachers' attitudes . . . were explored . . . in practice school governors will have the majority voice in deciding future staffing and their attitudes could be less positive than the heads' to extra support for the so-called 18 per cent. (Doyle and Rickman, 1989)

If section 19 were to be misused by headteachers, governors or LEAs we could witness the creation of an educational underclass divorced from the educational provision to which it is entitled and marginalized in a system which values competition and yet casts aside 'casualties' who are damaging to the public image. A primary school headteacher sums up the rising sense of alarm being felt by many practitioners:

Ultimately it is not profitable to impose a business model on an educational system. Children have differing strengths and needs and are a collective responsibility for us all. Proper performance measures are a priority, adequate funding is an essential and a closer look at the particular difficulties of budgets in primary schools is a matter of urgency. Most important of all is the commitment of everyone to equality of opportunity for all pupils, regardless of their ability or financial status. (Willey, 1989, p 138)

The new Act gives us a view of progression in a new order and inasmuch as this allows us to judge what it is that we must do to support a child it must be welcomed. However, we must ensure that *all* progress is celebrated.

Chapter Five
Local Management of Schools and Education Services

Ingrid Lunt

> Local Management of Schools represents a major challenge and a major
> opportunity for the education service. The introduction of needs-based
> formula-funding and the delegation of financial and managerial respon-
> sibilities to governing bodies are key elements in the Government's
> overall policy to improve the quality of teaching and learning in schools
> . . . the underlying principle of schemes of local management is to secure
> the maximum delegation . . . a limited number of services will continue
> to be provided centrally by the LEA, but only where that is clearly
> demonstrated to be more efficient or effective. (DES, 1988b, 9, 10)

By opening in this way, Circular 7/88 of the Education Reform Act
1988 states some of the key principles underlying this section of the Act,
and draws attention to the 'twin themes of local freedom and effective
management' (Mann, 1989). This chapter will consider some of the
aspects and possible implications of Local Management of Schools
(LMS) for the support of all pupils including those with special
educational needs and will look at some of the factors involved in the
organization of education support services and how these might fit into
a broader multidisciplinary framework.

LMS constitutes arguably the most significant and far-reaching
element of the reforms of the Education Reform Act. It coincides with
significant reforms in other public-sector provision and benefits from
consideration both in this context and in the context of a generally
changing background of local government. The education service is the
largest and most expensive service provided by local government; local
education authorities (LEAs) have over the past decade been subjected
to increasingly harsh criticism by the public, the media, the government
and particular agencies. Sheila Lawlor (1988) describes heads and

teachers as 'drawn into dependency on the LEA's social services [which] visibly sap individual initiative and responsibility and lead to mediocre uniformity'. There is no doubt that LMS is intended to curtail the power of LEAs and to 'tackle one of the most serious threats to education reform – the dominance of LEAs (and their doctrine of support services) in running the school system' (ibid).

Together with other provisions of the Education Reform Act, notably open enrolment and the National Curriculum assessment arrangements, financial delegation introduces the pressures of competition and the market economy to the provision of state education. Under open enrolment, schools will be required to take a maximum number of pupils and their size will therefore be determined by parental choice rather than, as hitherto, by LEA distribution of pupils across the schools of the authority. Since parents are likely to be substantially influenced in their choice of school by the publicly reported results of assessments at key stages 1, 2, 3 and 4, and it is in the financial interest of the school to attract as many pupils as possible, the package of reforms will force schools to compete with each other for pupils.

The question arises how far these principles can be made to fit in with the principles of equality of opportunity and the provision of high-quality education for *all* pupils. The past ten to 20 years have seen considerable developments in this field through legislation, social and educational policy and, to some extent, public awareness. A number of LEAs have sought to increase equality of opportunity for pupils regardless of ethnic background, gender and disability and to increase the range of opportunities available to children with special educational needs through integration within mainstream schools. How far is the 1988 Act compatible with these developments? John Welton suggests that:

> The Act overturns four decades of incremental development of the education system by the tripartite control and influence of central government, local government and the teaching profession . . . Policy for children with special educational needs emerged from separatism to incorporation such that the 1981 Act can be seen as the final part of the regulatory jigsaw designed to encourage local authorities and the professions to extend the comprehensive principle to all children. (Welton, 1989)

Under LMS, LEAs (except for Inner London) were required to submit proposals for financial delegation to the Secretary of State by

September 1989 and have these schemes fully in place in schools by April 1993. A three-stage annual budget process is proposed:

- Stage 1: LEA fixes the General Schools Budget, the total spending (direct and indirect) on all schools covered by the scheme, primary and secondary, for the financial year.
- Stage 2: LEA deducts from this the mandatory and discretionary 'excepted items'.
- Stage 3: This leaves the aggregated schools budget which is to be shared out to primary and secondary schools according to a formula (see below) as their budget share. (DES, 1988b)

The Coopers and Lybrand report (1988), from which the LMS arrangements are substantially derived, recommends that 'there will need to be a separate weighting factor for pupils with special educational needs' but gives no guidance as to how this complicated factor might be defined. Support for pupils with special educational needs is currently organized through various budgetary and organizational headings which range from the provision of separate special schools to the provision of central LEA support services whose main role is to support pupils with special needs in the ordinary school. These support services will be affected by two specific elements of the LMS arrangements: firstly, the nature and amount of 'discretionary exceptions' which may be retained centrally by the LEA; secondly, the nature of the 'formula' used to determine each school's budget share.

Discretionary exceptions
The discretionary exceptions for which the LEA may choose either to retain central responsibility or to delegate to schools include many which either specifically serve pupils with special educational needs – such as statements of special educational needs, some peripatetic/advisory teachers, special units – and others, such as educational psychologists and welfare officers who include these pupils among their wider concerns. Most LEAs are planning to retain these services centrally at present, but will face increased pressure to delegate them to schools since within three years the amount which may be retained from the list of discretionary exceptions will be reduced from 10 per cent to 7 per cent of the general schools budget. LMS poses an immediate threat to the provision of centrally coordinated education support services by the LEA and may thereby drive individual schools towards

a more piecemeal approach to supporting pupils which depends on an allocation of fractions of scarce resources to individual pupils.

Formula funding

LEAs are required to allocate to all schools in the scheme their share of the aggregated schools budget (ASB) on the basis of a 'formula' for which Circular 7/88 provides some guidelines: 'It will be for LEAs to determine the extent of variations in special needs between schools which should be taken into account in their formulae' (DES, 1988b). At least 75 per cent of the aggregated budget is to be allocated on the basis of age-weighted pupil numbers (AWPU); up to 25 per cent of ASB is to be allocated on the basis of other factors. Two factors may be expected to be included in the formula: special educational needs and curriculum protection for small schools, where appropriate. Several factors, such as variations in salary costs of small schools, non-statutory special needs, like social deprivation, premises costs (area, type, condition, other, eg, vandalism), are mentioned in the circular as factors which might be included. There is likely to be considerable variation in the percentages and formulae used by different LEAs (this has already been shown by the National Union of Teachers (NUT, 1989)) and this in turn will affect arrangements for the provision for pupils with special educational needs. Underpinning the scheme is the government's intention to:

- specify the unit costs of educational provision;
- attach the cost to the 'customer', ie the child (or rather parent);
- transfer this 'cost' (resource) to the school chosen.

This should remind us of the ill-fated 'voucher' scheme put forward by Sir Keith Joseph when Secretary of State in the early 1980s as a means of giving resources not to schools but to pupils (consumers) and thereby, under the guise of consumer (parental) choice, rewarding and resourcing schools which attracted the greatest numbers. The pressures of open enrolment and the National Curriculum assessment arrangements will force schools to compete for pupils, whose resourceworthiness has been specified by the budget, thus creating a potential upward or downward spiral for schools according to their popularity or otherwise, defined by the numbers of pupils that they are able to attract. How will this affect pupils with special educational needs? There is no doubt that there will be pressures on schools to avoid taking in pupils whose needs are outside 'the ordinary' unless they carry with them a sufficient extra resource to compensate for the extra demands which they make on the system.

It is early to look at the formulae and their implications, but a few pointers might be useful to illustrate some of the issues. In a recent survey, the majority of LEAs have a special needs factor as a weighting in the allocation, though this is frequently defined by oversimplified criteria such as free school meals or scores on a reading test. It is well known that such crude measures cannot adequately reflect the complexity of special educational needs amongst an LEA's pupils. It is also recognized that identification of pupils' needs involves a complex process requiring the assessment of a multiplicity of factors (DES, 1978). The percentage of budget allocated on the basis of AWPU (age weighted pupil numbers) ranged from 75 per cent (the permitted minimum) to 87 per cent with fewer authorities at the lower end of the range and therefore fewer authorities including a maximum weighting for other than age-weighted factors. The intention of the Act, to create competition between schools for pupil numbers who will 'pull their weight' in terms of assessment results is about to be realized. 'The hidden agenda of the ERA encourages the idea that pupils with special educational needs are a disadvantage to a school's results and, very importantly, to its use of teaching resources' (Willey, 1989).

Provision for pupils with special educational needs

LEAs currently spend a substantial sum on centrally provided and delivered support services for pupils with special educational needs. Within the LEA there is a network of professionals whose function is or includes direct or indirect support for these pupils. These include special needs advisers/inspectors, general advisers/inspectors, peripatetic teachers, educational social workers (welfare officers), educational psychologists, psychiatric social workers, special needs advisory and support teachers, home–school liaison teachers, preschool coordinators. These centrally provided education services are also required to work alongside the network of services provided by health and social services, with all the potential difficulties raised by interprofessional collaboration, communication, the possibilities of duplication and proliferation of efforts. Davies and Davies (1989) include the following among problems confronting administrators of such services:

- maximizing resources;
- dependency or ownership of responsibility;
- attitudinal change;

- the focus of support;
- collaboration and negotiation.

Although the 1981 Act specified that LEAs must operate 'within existing resources', the past decade has seen an enormous increase in the number and range of professionals supporting pupils with special educational needs. Gipps, Gross and Goldstein (1987) found wide regional variations in the nature of support services and a list of 35 different titles for services previously called 'remedial' and renamed as a result of the shift in conceptualization of special educational needs since the Warnock report. Moses, Hegarty and Jowett (1988) reported that a majority of authorities in their survey 'had achieved major changes in the structure and operation of their support services since 1978, and 20 per cent had taken the step of combining services to form a generic service as recommended in the Warnock report.' This period also showed a large increase in the number of educational psychologists, with a 40 per cent increase in their number between January 1981 and October 1986.

The Moses, Hegarty and Jowett survey (1988) found some confusion of role between the two major services concerned with pupils with special needs (special education service and psychological service) and pointed out the need for 'coordination and cooperation at all levels between the different agencies to avoid unnecessary duplication of services to some schools and the possibility of conflicting advice.' A further survey of LEAs and the workings of the 1981 Act (Goacher et al, 1987) found 52 per cent of LEAs reporting a substantial increase in the number of support personnel available to work with children with special needs and a 'substantial increase in the proportion of children with special educational needs receiving education in mainstream schools.' It is clear therefore that LEA services concerned with supporting pupils with special educational needs in a range of ways on a continuum of provision – much of it in mainstream schools – have increased since the 1981 Act, though for some LEAs this very wealth and range has led to some confusion and lack of coordination among the different services:

> There can be drawbacks in having numerous sources of advice. The support received by schools risks being fragmented, and teachers may be confused by conflicting emphases and aproaches. From the providers' viewpoint, the separation between services means that there is little

coordination between them, and it is unlikely that best use is made of scarce resources. (Hegarty, 1987)

Further, a recent HMI survey of support services identified problems of coordination and inadequate leadership in many of the LEAs surveyed. (DES, 1989)

For such reasons the Warnock report recommended the establishment of unified services. In addition, with the growing awareness by those concerned with special needs of the *relative* and *interactive* nature of special educational needs and the realization that school organization, culture and curriculum are important factors influencing pupils' learning outcomes there have been exhortations towards whole-school policies, both for special needs and other areas (Thomas and Feiler, 1988; Ainscow and Florek, 1989). Yet, as Dessent (1987) points out, the vast majority of education support services retain the traditional features:

- individual/referral orientated;
- referral to an expert;
- definers of 'specialness' or 'resourceworthiness';
- high priority given to assessment;
- no requirement for resource/organisational change in the school.

In this way centrally provided services are still predominantly linked to individual pupils. There may at first sight be good reason for this. Dessent (ibid) mentions the phenomenon of 'resource drift' when 'resources which have been specifically earmarked for low-status special needs are often diverted and redirected unless "protected" in some way within the "marketplace" of the ordinary school system.' He continues:

> Practices such as these indicate perhaps an underlying value system which upholds the view that priority for resources in the educational system should go to the potential wealth providers (academically able pupils), rather than to pupils who are seen as contributing little to the future economic prosperity of the nation. Arguably, what we have, in mainstream education, is a system of positive discrimination for the most able pupils in our schools (ibid, p 15).

The potential for positive discrimination for the most able pupils must ring particular alarm bells for those concerned with pupils with

special educational needs in the light of the pressures on schools
brought by the 1988 Act.

The 2 per cent and the 18 per cent

How should the 'resourceworthiness' of (different) special educational
needs be defined? Circular 1/83 (DES, 1983) (and the recent Circular
22/89 (DES, 1989b)) endorsed the earlier distinction between 'special'
and 'ordinary' or between 'segregated' and 'non-segregated' by the
statementing process

> where there are prima-facie grounds to suggest that a child's needs are
> such as to require provision additional to, or otherwise different from,
> the facilities and resources generally available in ordinary schools in the
> area under normal arrangements.

The definition of the prima-facie case (and therefore the 'resourceworthiness') is a difficult and relative matter and depends on a range of
factors, many of which may have little to do with the pupil herself. 'The
greatest difficulty which arises from the concept of relativity is how to
define the characteristics of a reasonable educational programme
generally available in schools in a local education authority area' (Fish,
1989).

There is wide regional variation in the percentage of children who
have statements and therefore protected resources (Swann, 1985), with
a national average of about 1.7 per cent of children having statements
and of these, about a quarter being educated in ordinary schools. What
is clear is that it is often a somewhat arbitrary decision whether a pupil
is among the 2 per cent of those with protected resources or among the
18 per cent who are recognized as having special educational needs but
who have no specifically allocated resources and may be dependent on
the support, direct or indirect, from one of the central LEA support
services. This continuum from direct to indirect support is now well
known, yet it is possible to ask, with Dyer (1988) 'Whom is the support
teacher supporting? The child, the teacher, the family or the curriculum?' One could add 'the school, the LEA, the system?' Whatever the
answer, the issue remains that it has so far been difficult to define or to
quantify the cost of this support:

> Special needs provision may be receiving a variety of inputs from
> education–school psychological service, advisory support team, educa-
> tion welfare officers, transport – plus medical and paramedical services

from health, and social work input from social services. Information has to be extracted from all of these sources in order to give a full picture (Hegarty, 1987).

On the other hand, the statemented provision is relatively easier to cost. Its resource-based and individually focused nature means that a statemented pupil will either cost the authority a special-school placement of up to three times the cost of an ordinary school place (1987–8 figures: £4925 special school, £1010 primary, £1520 secondary; source: 'Special Education in Parliament', *British Journal of Special Education*, 1989), or may be deemed to deserve a specified number of individual support hours in the mainstream school. This process assumes that if it were possible and desirable to identify those pupils who (according to agreed educational, social, economic, ethical criteria) deserved greater resources because of their greater need or deservedness, these pupils could in theory carry with them this enhanced 'value' as they moved about the school system.

How does this fit with the 1988 Act and in particular with LMS? Special schools are currently excluded from LMS though LEAs may delegate their budget if they wish. Statemented pupils are in the list of discretionary exceptions subject to the 10 per cent limit, and most LEAs this year propose to retain provision for statementing centrally. Few LEAs will therefore yet have to face the question of what it means to delegate and to cost statementing (both the process and the provision) and the implications for the schools concerned. The government's expenditure plans for 1989–90 provided for LEAs to spend £59 million – or over 10 per cent more – in cash on maintained special schools than in 1988–89; 'NCC does not expect the demands of the National Curriculum to lead to a rise in numbers of pupils assessed for statements under the 1981 Act' (NCC, 1989a). Nevertheless there may be a temptation for schools to put forward more pupils for statutory assessment either in order to attract more resources to the school or to transfer pupils to special schools in order for them to appear outside the assessment reporting for the ordinary school. The DES booklet *From Policy to Practice* (DES, 1989a) contains an alarmingly 'reassuring' paragraph on this issue which permits schools not to publish school-based information about results of assessments for pupils with special educational needs: 'That way schools need have no fear that the overall picture of attainment for their pupils will suffer because children with special educational needs are included.' Indeed a headteacher might wish to insist that s/he would take in a child with special educational needs only if that child had a statement and therefore brought with her extra resources.

A question arises, then, do *all* children have the right of access to their local school – the right to the resources which will enable them to participate in the broad and balanced curriculum alongside their peers? If so, how are these resources to be distributed? In theory it would be possible to calculate the costs of additional resources for special educational needs in the same way as age-weighted pupil numbers costs are now calculated, and to go further and assign different amounts to different 'types' of need which the statemented (or non-statemented) child would bring to whichever school s/he attends. In practice this raises the difficulties of individual identification, individual categorization and individual focus rather than the continuum of need, and encourages an individual approach to resourcing which goes against many of the recent developments in thinking about support for special educational needs. Yet it is clear that the 1988 Act places pressure on schools, headteachers and governing bodies to adopt a highly individualistic approach to the allocation of resources to meet the needs of all pupils in the school.

The disadvantages of this approach are clear. The separation of the special education budget from the ordinary school budget in order to protect the former has led to a predominantly separate resourcing of special educational needs either in the form of

● special school placement;
● specified resources in the ordinary school through a statement;
● support, often of a less specified kind, for the '18 per cent' of children in ordinary schools.

It has proved much less easy to resource schools for 'whole-school approaches' or indeed to create the situation in which resources originally allocated in respect of one or two individual pupils are used both to improve the learning environment of the whole school and simultaneously to support those children who originally attracted the 'extra' resources. Under LMS, if the costs of providing support for the 18 per cent who might have special needs in ordinary schools are to be delegated to schools, there are several immediate dangers. These include the possibility that the resources are immediately so reduced as to be difficult to deploy, that the resources may either 'drift' away from the intended recipient or, if protected, provide segregation away from mainstream activities; and that the devolution of resources encourages an individual-child rather than a whole-school or a curricular approach: 'The "market forces model" whereby schools attract increased funding through enrolling more pupils, ignores the support mechanisms built up over many years by local education authorities, for sound educational reasons' (Darlington, 1989).

The present arrangements, with the pressures of LMS open enrolment and the National Curriculum, demand even more urgently 'the development of a unified support service to schools and colleges which specifies what it can deliver, where, how often and at what cost' (Fish, 1989). John Fish suggests a number of dimensions by which a support service for pupils with special educational needs might be defined, and levels of intervention which might help to calculate the cost. Each of the dimensions 'represents a continuum from an attribute of everyday education through an increasing modification of that attribute to the variation necessary to educate a child with the most severe and complex special educational needs' (ibid). The dimensions are grouped as situational, temporal, professional teaching, supporting professional and parental, and might be used to specify in detail the level of support needed by an individual pupil with special educational needs.

Faced with the alternatives of delegation of support resources to schools and central retention of support services, it may be helpful to consider an 'intermediate' type of organization which is gaining some interest among LEAs. This is the cluster arrangement (ILEA, 1985a and 1985b) which involves a group of schools collaborating and pooling a share of their delegated resources in order to counteract the disadvantages of considerably reduced decentralized resources scattered between individual schools and to develop a collaborative approach to meeting pupils' needs. These shared resources might be used to support any of the dimensions suggested by Fish above. Further, it is suggested that support services could usefully operate within a cluster arrangement which had as its focus a group of schools and their locality and community, such that a unified education support service, organized around a cluster of schools, worked closely with a local social-services and health-service provision in order to maximize the efficient and effective use of scarce resources to support young people with special needs, both at school age and at pre-school and post-16. The benefits of this system are obvious: interdisciplinary collaboration, continuity of services across age phases and across professional boundaries, a model of collaboration giving schools support in the absence of that provided by the LEA, and a possibility of directing support to locally identified needs from a team familiar with the context of the locality and its schools. Several LEAs are arranging cluster groupings for different purposes and it remains to be seen how far schools will be willing or able to pool resources after LMS in order to support their pupils with special educational needs. It may be difficult to see the incentives or rewards for schools when confronted with the pressures of LMS.

The threats to support for children with special educational needs
If we return to the 'twin themes of local freedom and effective management' (Mann, 1989) it is possible to see some of the threats posed to support for children with special educational needs. The 1988 Act comes at a time of decreased public spending with demands for increased accountability and productivity. For education services, productivity is defined in terms of standards: 'the government's central aim is to improve standards in schools, using the available resources to yield the best possible return' (DES, 1985) and 'the National Curriculum will give a clear incentive for weaker schools to catch up with the best and the best will be challenged to do even better' (NCC, 1989a). The problem is that children with special needs do not immediately 'yield the best return' and therefore the protection of services to support such pupils will not necessarily be seen as a high priority. In an already over-stretched education service and its very over-stretched schools, with schools explicitly competing for pupil numbers on the basis of 'good results' will there be room for pupils with special educational needs and will schools be able to support them? Forced to make choices between the conflicting priorities of support for more able pupils (less demanding of resources and more 'cost-effective') and for pupils with special needs, schools and their governors, even if willing, may not be able to 'afford' to make suitable and expensive provision for *all* children (including those individuals and small groups with special needs) to have access to a broad and balanced curriculum at their local school.

> The main impact of the 1988 Education Reform Act on the needs of children with special educational needs is likely to come from its long-term effects on the shape of the whole education system. Increased fragmentation of the governance of schools will destroy any possibility of strategic planning by LEAs to meet the needs of minority groups . . . The uncontrollable impact of market forces operating on an increasingly disintegrated pattern of educational provision is likely to severely reduce provision for all children with special educational needs. (Welton, 1989, p 26)

Under these circumstances it is imperative for LEAs and for services to develop unified policies and services, to define what kind of support is offered and at what cost and to be prepared to develop strategies within the new framework which will enable schools to meet the needs, rights and entitlement of all children to a fully comprehensive education.

Chapter Six
Support Services for Children with Language and Communication Difficulties

Jannet Wright

Children who have communication problems are a heterogeneous group. Communication problems cover a wide spectrum of difficulty and are characterized by deficits in understanding, verbal expression and use of language. Language difficulties may be conceptualized as a continuum of difficulty and so the terminology used in the literature to describe a child with a communication problem is varied and confusing. In this chapter the term 'communication problem' will be used to include the whole continuum of speech and language problems.

Communication problems may be identified at an early age. In fact, certain structural abnormalities or neurological conditions such as a cleft palate or cerebral palsy make it more likely that a child will have difficulties which will require speech-therapy intervention. Others will be identified either when language skills fail to develop in the expected way, or at developmental checks in the pre-school years. For some children the problem will not be recognized until they enter school.

A child whose language difficulties were identified in the pre-school years will, therefore, already be known at school entry to at least one support service, namely speech therapy. This support service is an important provision for children with such a special educational need.

Speech-therapy provision
The range of services provided by speech therapy includes assessment and information on both developmental and acquired disorders of communication, and therapeutic intervention on a regular basis. If the child's communication difficulty is identified after school entry, the referral to speech therapy may be part of a coordinated response by the school to an individual child's special educational needs.

The majority of speech therapists are employed by the National

Health Service. Arrangements for service provision to language units, units for the hearing impaired and special schools are the concern of the district speech-therapy manager (DSTM). The DSTM is responsible for the appointment of speech-therapy staff and the planning of service delivery to both education and health-service establishments.

The response of the local education authority (LEA) and the district health authority (DHA) to the needs of a child with a communication problem vary from region to region. This variation in response is exacerbated further by the fact that the LEA and DHA boundaries are not always coterminous.

The fact that most speech therapy posts are funded from the health authority means that therapists working with school-age children are having to deal with the implications of the government White Papers on the health service at the same time as the Education Reform Act. Reorganization of the health service may lead to considerable variation within each health-authority district. This could mean significant changes in the way speech therapy services are organized and funded.

For school-age children with communication problems, the recent High Court rulings have not done anything to clarify the situation about whether speech therapy is an educational or non-educational provision. This situation is restated in Circular 22/89:

> In the case of speech therapy provision LEAs should be aware that the High Court case of R v Lancashire County Council ex parte CM (March 1989) ruled that speech therapy provision could be considered as either educational or non-educational provision. (DES, 1989b Para. 63)

The implications of this paragraph are to allow LEAs to employ speech therapists if they wish to.

The communication impaired child

Without a statement
The majority of children seen by speech therapists do not have a statement. They may be referred because their teacher, parent of doctor is concerned about the development of their speech and language. Speech therapy for some children may only be necessary for a short period of time. For other children it will be a necessary support throughout their school life. Speech therapy may take place in a health centre or in school. If the child is seen in school the therapist may work with the child in the classroom or take the child out of the class.

Although it can be very beneficial to see a child in the classroom, especially to help the development of functional communication skills, many children are taken out of school to attend speech therapy. This is often due to local DHA policy. A speech therapist is required to complete Korner statistical returns, indicating the number of people seen and type of management offered. By spending a whole morning in a clinic the therapist can probably see three or four children but a whole morning spent visiting a school to see one child and one teacher may not look as productive to a DHA administrator.

However, for the child with a communication problem, an appointment at the speech-therapy clinic may mean that half a day of school is missed. It also makes it more difficult for the teacher and therapist to offer a coordinated approach to the child's needs. This can make it difficult to ensure that children with a communication problem are getting the quality of the support that they require.

With the introduction of the National Curriculum, even when therapists are not working directly in the school situation they have the opportunity, at least in theory, of knowing what the requirements of the curriculum will be. This may make it easier to plan therapy programmes which are more relevant to the child's classroom activities.

The prominence given to oracy in the English curriculum has been welcomed by those working with children who have communication problems. The Kingman report (DES, 1988c), the National Oracy Project (NCC, 1987) and the Language in the Curriculum project (LINC), have all brought with them terminology and a vocabulary which up until now have been seen by teachers as 'jargon'. These projects, along with the English curriculum, will influence teachers' thinking about language and thus communication. Both therapists and teachers will be sharing common terms such as syntax and pragmatics. The availability of all these documents for public consumption should facilitate shared terminology and thus inter-professional communication. This should produce a positive outcome for the child with special educational needs.

Many language-impaired children may have great difficulty with the attainment targets in speaking and listening. Teachers will therefore be more aware of problems in this area and may wish to make more referrals to speech therapy or ask for greater speech therapy support in school.

If such children do not have statements and schools are not able to provide in-school support for them, or if the DHA reorganizes service delivery so that all communication-impaired children have to come to a clinic, a conflict of interests may arise. Teachers are going to be concerned if the child has to spend half a day travelling to a clinic and so misses part of the curriculum on which they will later be assessed. Does this mean that a child who needs speech therapy will have to have a statement in order to attend a speech-therapy clinic? And will provision be made in school for them to catch up with missed work?

With a statement
Since the 1981 Education Act more posts have been created for speech therapists to work in mainstream schools or support statemented children in the mainstream. Sometimes parental pressure on the DHA has resulted in the creation of a new post. A child from a mainstream school with a communication problem and a statement may be seen by a therapist who spends the majority of his or her time in a health clinic seeing children who are accompanied by their parents, as happens with those who do not have statements. Other therapists may use the clinic as an administrative base and spend most of the day in school. Children who attend language units, units for the hearing impaired or special schools may be seen by speech therapists who are based in that school or unit.

When teachers and therapists are based in the same place information about children with communication problems can easily be exchanged. This has not always been the case when a child attends a mainstream school. In the past, teachers of children with communication problems did not always receive a full report from the speech therapist when a statement of a child's need was being prepared. This was because the medical officer preparing the medical evidence sometimes included only selected portions from the report. In paragraph 42 of Circular 22/89, it is stated that advice about all therapy services provided by the DHA should be passed 'in full' to the LEA and attached as an appendix (DES, 1989b). So now headteachers and class teachers should have full details of the child's needs from the speech therapist's viewpoint.

Implications for children with communication problems under the Education Reform Act
If the needs of a child with a communication problem are to be met successfully then the speech therapist and teacher need to collaborate over their approach to ensure continuity. This may happen successfully in the classroom environment where links with the teaching staff will

help to ensure the generalization of newly acquired language skills. This professional collaboration is supported in Circular 22/89:

> Effective multi-professional work requires cooperation, collaboration and mutual support on the part of the contributors. (DES, 1989b, para 51)

However, under Local Management of Schools (LMS) this continuity and consistency could be in question. If schools with limited budgets have to buy speech therapy time from the DHA, will they want to have a therapist who is on the premises for part of the week and thus has some time to collaborate with teaching staff or will the school be looking for minimum contact time with the language-impaired child?

Unless a support service has made its expertise clear and has marketed itself well, headteachers will be at a loss to know which services to approach when seeking advice about a child with communication problems. The choice may be based on personal contacts rather than an informed assessment of the child's needs and the services available to meet these needs.

Speech therapists are becoming aware of the potential influence of school governors. They are beginning to target these people to ensure that the needs of communication-impaired children are understood and how speech therapists can help to meet the needs of these children. Support for this move may be found in Circular 22/89:

> There remains a need for LEAs and governors to take steps to satisfy parents of children without statements that appropriate educational provision will be available in schools to meet their particular needs. Schools should publish information for parents indicating their special-support provision for children with SEN, but with no statements. (Ibid., para 16)

The influence of school governors may be crucial in deciding whether children who have been placed in a language unit because of the severity of their communication problem will continue to have that specialist environment. Units attached to mainstream schools may find that they are threatened with closure under LMS. If children from units are to be transferred back into mainstream classes then there must be concern about the availability and access to teachers with specialized knowledge about communication problems.

The government White Papers on the reorganization of the health service will have implications for school budgets. Previously speech therapists have worked in schools without anyone being aware of the real costs. District speech therapy managers are currently carrying out costing exercises which will aim to charge users the real costs of speech-therapy sessions. When a school is aware of the services that speech therapy can provide, it is hoped that the financial costs will not be viewed as too great.

Conclusion

Children with communication problems require the help of both teachers and speech therapists. Changes in the way such children are supported will be inevitable following the 1988 Education Act. It will need considerable innovation and communication to maintain the support they need. The speech therapy profession spends a large amount of time with children of school age. It is trying not only to be responsive to government initiatives but to develop the services children need in a positive and innovative way.

Conclusion

Harry Daniels and Jean Ware

The sheer volume of circulars, guidelines and other documents issued by the Department of Education and Science, the National Curriculum Council and the Schools Examination and Assessment Council about the National Curriculum alone, is, to say the least, overwhelming for teachers, governors and local education authority officers alike.

It is also clear that there is much more to the Education Reform Act than the National Curriculum. The complexity of the interactions between the implementation of the National Curriculum and the changes in the systems of school management and funding make it difficult to predict the eventual outcomes for children with special educational needs. However, we believe that one possible way to influence these outcomes positively is by alerting as wide a group as possible to the dangers. We hope that this volume will make some contribution to this process.

By way of conclusion it is perhaps worth summarizing some of our major reservations. The restraining influence of the prescribed elements of the National Curriculum on matching provision to need is a concern which requires urgent attention. Successful implementation of the 1988 Act for children with special educational needs will involve discussion of the appropriate balance between general entitlement and individual need within the *whole* curriculum. If modification or disapplication is to be sought, the rationale must be clearly linked to individual rather than system need. However, it is too simple to suggest, as has been done in the context of implementation of the National Curriculum for children with severe learning difficulties (National Curriculum Development Team, 1990) that *all* modifications are against the interests of children with special needs.

We most certainly need more clarity about what modification means in practice. If exemption were to become relegation to some kind of educational wilderness used to service the marketing needs of the school, then it would have to be resisted. If it were to be used to enable schools to deliver an appropriately balanced and differentiated curriculum then it could arguably be seen as a way of providing for a wide range of special educational needs needs within a sensitive and supportive framework. In the same way if the idea of exempting children with special educational needs from the assessments arrangements is used merely to hide low attainment then it too must be resisted. If, on the other hand, it leads to the development of procedures for monitoring individual progress which provide teachers with relevant curriculum-based information then it could lead to a wider use of what is currently recognized as good practice. Such dissemination of good practice is, of course, one the aims of the Education Reform Act.

The systems of financial management and accountability introduced by the 1988 act are open to abuse. This abuse could be directed at children with special educational needs. The rhetoric of competition between schools could create a harsh market culture within which children with special needs become educational 'wastage'. However, if schools were to exercise this opportunity for managing their own affairs by cooperating with other schools to share scarce resources and develop collective responses to community needs, then this 'wastage', which is so expensive in human terms, could be avoided. Similarly, cooperation between statutory services could be stifled, by 'real-cost' accounting.

There are, of course, many positive features in the Act. The notion of entitlement is, for example, one which could be developed and refined. This would enable the stated aims of the Act to be achieved by all children, whatever their circumstances.

It is clear to us that there is a need to establish a positive approach to the implementation of the Act. Experience of good practice following the 1981 Act has shown that it is possible to create a system of curriculum development, pedagogy, assessment and accountability which will enable all educational needs to be met. The framework of the 1988 Act could also be interpreted in this way, if there is the social and political will.

Appendix
Special Cases within the 1988 Education Reform Act: A Digest of Sections 16, 17, 18 and 19

These four sections detail the possibilities afforded for the disapplication and modification of the National Curriculum within the 1988 Act.

Section 16
This section enables development work or experiments to be carried out. It may be applied generally or in particular cases at the request of either the governing body, the local education authority (in agreement with the governing body) or the National Curriculum Council (with the agreement of both). Whoever requests the use of section 16 may be required to make regular reports to the Secretary of State. Section 16 may only be used in county, controlled or maintained *special* schools and grant-maintained, aided or special agreement schools.

Section 17
This section allows for the disapplication and modification of the National Curriculum in specific cases or circumstances. It allows for group application.

Section 18
This section allows for the disapplication or modification of the requirements of the National Curriculum in the case of individual pupils for whom a statement of special educational need has been made under section 7 of the 1981 Act.

Section 19
This section allows for a headteacher temporarily to disapply or modify the requirements of the National Curriculum for individual pupils. It

details the conditions under which it may apply and the requirements for notification of parents, governors and local education authorities along with outline appeal procedures. Local education authorities are required to consider whether action is required in order to assess the child's special educational needs under section 5 of the 1981 Act. The Secretary of State reserves the right to make relevant consultations before making any reservations under this section.

References

Ainscow, M. and Florek, A. (1989), *Special Educational Needs: Towards a Whole School Approach*, London: David Fulton Pub. and National Council for Special Education.

Coopers & Lybrand (1988), *Local Management of Schools – a report to the Department of Education and Science*, London: HMSO.

Darlington, S. (1989), Letter to the editor, *British Journal of Special Education* 16, 4, 169.

Davies, J.D. and Davies, P. (1989), *A Teacher's Guide to Support Services*, Windsor: NFER-Nelson.

DES (1978), *Special Educational Needs* (Warnock Report), Cmnd 7212, London: HMSO.

DES (1983), *Circular 1/83, Assessments and Statements of Special Educational Needs: Procedures within the Education, Health and Social Services*, London: DES.

DES (1985), *Better Schools*, Cmnd, 9469. London: HMSO.

DES (1988a), *Education Reform Act 1988*, London: DES

DES (1988b), *Circular 7/88: Education Reform Act: Local Management of Schools*, London: DES.

DES (1988c), *Report of the (Kingman) Committee of Inquiry into the Teaching of English Language*, London: HMSO.

DES (1989a), *From Policy to Practice*, London: DES.

DES (1989b), *Circular 22/89: Assessments and Statements of Special Educational Needs: Procedures within the Education, Health and Social Services*, London: DES.

DES (1989c), *Circular 6/89: The Education Reform Act: National Curriculum: Mathematics and Science Orders under Section 4*, London: DES.

DES (1989d), *Circular 15/89: Education Reform Act 1988: Temporary

Exceptions to the National Curriculum, (also regulations), London: DES.

DES (1989e), *Circular 1/89: Education Reform Act 1988: Local Arrangements for the Consideration of Complaints*, London DES.

DES (1989f), *Report by HM Inspectors on a Survey of Support Services for Special Educational Needs*, London: DES.

Dessent, T. (1987), *Making the Ordinary School Special*, Lewes: Falmer Press.

Doe, B. (1989), 'To market, to market, to sell a fine school', *Times Educational Supplement* 15.2.89.

Doyle, P. and Rickman, R. (1989), 'LMS: Implications for the 18 per cent', *British Journal of Special Education* 15, 2, 77–79.

Dyer, C. (1988), 'Which support? an examination of the term', *Support for Learning* 3, 1, 6–11.

Education Act (1944), London: HMSO

Education (Handicapped) Children Act (1970), London: HMSO.

Education Act (1981), London HMSO.

Education Reform Act (1988), London: HMSO.

Evans, P. and Ware, J. (1987), *Special Care Provision: The Education of Children with Profound and Multiple Learning Difficulties*, Windsor: NFER-Nelson.

Feuerstein, R., Rand, Y., and Hoffman, M.B. (1979), *The Dynamic Assessment of Retarded Performers. The Learning Potential Assessment Device*, New York: University Park Press.

Fish, J. (1989), *What is Special Education?*, Milton Keynes: Open University Press.

Fish, J., Mongon, D., Evans, P. and Wedell, K. (1987 and 1988), *Memorandum to the DES in Response to the Consultation Document on The National Curriculum*, London: London University, Institute of Education.

Fordham, D. (1989), 'Flexibility in the National Curriclum', *British Journal of Special Education* 16, 2, 50–52.

Gipps, C., Gross, H., and Goldstein, H. (1987), *Warnock's Eighteen Per Cent*, Lewes: Falmer Press.

Goacher, B., Evans, J., Welton, J. and Wedell, K. (1988), *Policy and Provision for Special Educational Need. Implementing the 1981 Act*, London: Cassell.

Hegarty, S., (1987), *Special Needs in Ordinary Schools*, London: Cassell.

ILEA (1985a), *Improving Primary Schools*, London: ILEA.

ILEA (1985b), *Educational Opportunities for All/The Report of the*

Committee Reviewing Provision to meet Special Educational Needs (The Fish Report), London: ILEA.

Lawlor, S. (1988), *Away with LEAs: ILEA Abolition as a Pilot*, London: Centre for Policy Studies.

LINC (1988), *Languages in the Curriculum*, Project Report, Leeds: University of Leeds

Longhorn, F. (1988), *Planning a Sensory Curriculum for Very Special People*, Souvenir Press.

Mann, J. (1989), in 'Week by Week', *Education*, 8 December 1989.

Moses, D., Hegarty, S., and Jowett, S. (1988), *Supporting Ordinary Schools: LEA Initiatives*, Windsor: NFER-Nelson.

NCC (1987), *National Oracy Project*, Planning Brief NCC.

NCC (1989a), *Curriculum Guidance Number 2: A Curriculum for All Special Educational Needs in the National Curriculum*, York: NCC.

NCC (1989b), *Circular Number 5. Implementing the NC. Participation by pupils with SEN*, York: NCC.

National Curriculum Development Team (Severe Learning Difficulties) (1990), Newsletter One, February, Cambridge: Cambridge Institute of Education.

Norwich, B. (1989), 'How should we define exceptions?', *British Journal of Special Education* 16, 3, 94–97.

Norwich, B. (1990), *Reappraising Special Needs Education*, London: Cassell (in press).

NUT (1989), *Education Reform Act 1988: Local Management of Schools*, London: NUT.

Peter, M. (1989), 'Exceptions from the National Curriculum', *British Journal of Special Education* 16, 2, 49.

Schools Examination and Assessment Council (1989), 'National Curriculum Assessment and Testing', Ref MRF/PUB 6/1 (a statement by SEAC).

Schools Examination and Assessment Council (1990), *A Guide to Teacher Assessment*, London: Heineman Educational.

Swann, W. (1985), 'Is the integration of children with special needs happening?' (an analysis of recent statistics of pupils in special schools) *Oxford Review of Education* 2, 1, 3–18.

Thomas, G and Feiler, A., eds (1988), *Planning for Special Needs: A Whole School Approach*, Oxford: Basil Blackwell.

Tilstone, C. (1989), 'Rana's Day', unpublished Inset material, Birmingham: Westhill College.

Tilstone, C. and Steel, A (1989), 'National Curriculum severe learning difficulties, West Midlands Monitoring Group', Briefing Paper 3, Birmingham: Westhill College.

Ware, J. (1989), 'The National Curriculum and children with profound and multiple learning difficulties', paper presented to an invited seminar at Castle Priory College, Wallingford, September 1989. Available from the author at The Institute of Education, University of London.

Wedell, K., Evans, J., Goacher, B. and Welton, J. (1987), 'The 1981 Education Act: Policy and Provision for Special Educational Needs', *British Journal of Special Education* 14, 2, 50–53.

Welton, J. (1989), 'Incrementalism to Catastrophe Theory', in C. Roaf and H. Bines, (eds), *Needs, Rights and Opportunities*, Lewes: Falmer Press.

Willey, M. (1989), 'LMS: A rising sense of alarm', *British Journal of Special Education* 16, 4, 136–138.

Index